Caste, Reservation, Atrocity Law and Discrimination

Caste, Reservation, Atrocity Law and Discrimination

Sthabir Khora

AAKAR

Caste, Reservation, Atrocity Law and Discrimination
Sthabir Khora

First Published 2020
Reprinted 2022

ISBN 978-93-5002-660-1

Published by
AAKAR BOOKS
28 E Pocket IV, Mayur Vihar Phase I
Delhi 110 091 India
aakarbooks@gmail.com

Laser Typeset at
Arpit Printographers, Delhi

Printed at
Sapra Brothers, Noida

Contents

Abbreviations and Glossary

ASI	Assistant Sub Inspector
CA	Chartered Accountant
CBI	Central Bureau of Investigation
CPC	Civil Procedure Code
CrPC	Criminal Procedure Code
CSR	Corporate Social Responsibility
EU	European Union
GDP	Gross Domestic Product
HR	Human Resource
IAS	Indian Administrative Service
IIT	Indian Institute of Technology
IPC	Indian Penal Code
IPS	Indian Police Service
MLA	Member of Legislative Assembly
MP	Member of Parliament
MSP	Minimum Support Price
NCRB	National Crime Records Bureau
NGO	Non-Government Organisation
NPA	Non-Performing Asset
NRI	Non-Resident Indian
OBC	Other Backward Classes
PCR	Protection of Civil Rights Act (1955)
POA/ Atrocities Act	Schedule Caste and Scheduled Tribe (Prevention of Atrocities) Act 1989
RSS	Rashtriya Swayam Sewak Sangh

RTE	Right to Education Act 2009
SC	Scheduled Caste
SCP	Special Component Plant
SSP	Senior Superintendent of Police
ST	Scheduled Tribe
UK	United Kingdom
UP	Uttar Pradesh
USA	United States of America
USSR	Union of Soviet Socialist Republics

Preface

The purpose of this book is to bring in one place my articles scattered in *Economic and Political Weekly* and *Round Table India* along with some hitherto unpublished ones so that the reader gets in one place these articles on interrelated themes of caste, reservation, atrocity law and discrimination. The debate around these issues has been revolving in a rather fixed manner. The essays here do some free thinking on these issues, make a combination of existing theories and suggest a way out on particular issues. For example, many have tried to defend reservation in the private sector, but that does not shatter the sanctity of the 'private' which needs to be penetrated if we are to justify reservation in the private sector. Similarly, discussions on the 'creamy layer' do not get into the tension between individual rights and group rights and therefore they land in some sort of impasse.

I am thankful to the *Economic and Political Weekly* and *Round Table India* for giving me permission to reproduce my articles originally published by them. I owe gratitude to Aakar Books and Shri K.K. Saxena for publishing this collection.

This book, I hope, will be useful to the academic community as well as to the general readers.

February 2020 **Sthabir Khora**

1

Introduction

The book consists of three parts focussing on three interrelated issues—caste, reservation, and the atrocity law. The first part deals with some of the contentious theoretical issues about caste. The Second chapter highlights the power aspect of the caste system and speculates its possible role in the origin and sustenance of caste. We already have speculations on religious, racial and occupational origin of caste. But they are unsatisfactory. Religious origin cannot explain the *shudra* acceptance of their lowest place merely on the basis of shastra. From time to time the *shudra*s have acquired power and declared or got themselves declared as *kshatriya* whenever they found an opportunity. This is not what the *shastra*s have prescribed as their *dharma*. Racial theory of the origin of caste cannot explain the relative hierarchy between the *kshatriya* and *brahman* when both can be considered to belong to the same race. Similarly, occupational theory cannot explain the lack of freedom of occupations in India historically. In contrast to this, the contribution of political power to the origin of caste has not been much highlighted so far. If we speculate that it is political power that gave rise to caste then the practical implication is that it is power that holds the key for the marginalised to deal with caste.

The next chapter deals with an important academic strategy for undermining caste—roping in the intellectual elite to dwell on caste. The intellectual elite can maintain their moral high ground by either remaining silent or giving lukewarm support to anti-caste arguments under the cover of 'intellectual freedom', thereby keeping their liberal admirers intact. But, from a pragmatic point of view, it helps to rope in them rather than dismiss them. Chapter Three tries to do this by roping in Amartya Sen to substantiate caste as an unjust system. Amartya Sen is primarily known as an eminent philosopher rather than a sociologist. But when we deal with caste as a justice issue, it is difficult to avoid Amartya Sen who has written on justice. It is definitely better to have his writing for a critique of caste because the Indian and global liberals are more likely to pay heed to him. Though it is possible to dismiss him as someone who has not written much on caste and therefore is not a scholar on caste, it makes sense to bring him in as a justice theorist for a critique of caste. This chapter starts by pointing out how Amartya Sen has not taken much recognition of caste in his writing. But later it brings in useful ideas from his book *The Idea of Justice* (2010) for a critique of caste.

The next two Chapters—Four and Five—deal with the scope of inter-caste marriage and religious conversion in destroying caste in the backdrop of liberalism. Many have reposed faith in inter-caste marriage's potential to weaken caste. The only hurdle seems to be the violent backlash. Chapter Four discusses the theoretical limit of inter-caste marriage's potential to destroy caste. Inter-caste marriage, that is also 'arranged', has the potential to weaken caste as it assumes group agreement—the agreement between the bride and the groom side. However, theoretically, there cannot be an inter-caste marriage that is also 'arranged' because it presupposes the loosening of the stranglehold of caste on the society. On the other hand, love marriage, which assumes liberal individualism, cannot solve the corporate problem of caste just like individual friendship between an upper and a lower caste cannot weaken caste as a system.

Chapter Five deals with the puzzle of getting out of caste in the context of religious conversion. Experience shows that religious conversion does not destroy caste in India. Caste is present across religious communities in India though it is not sanctioned by any except by Hindu religious scriptures. Interestingly the solution to this puzzle is inspired by a dialogue in a Hollywood movie. There is a memorable quote in the Hollywood movie *The International* by the character Cassian Skarssen (played by Benjamin Wandschneider)—'When there's no way out, you find a deeper way in'. Sometimes we need to change the paradigm to find a solution. The thrust of this article is that instead of trying to get out of the caste completely, which is not possible in a liberal framework, we should try to minimize the damage as far as possible through the law.

Caste has so far been at the receiving end of a top-down theorising. Chapter Six tries to reverse this by some sort of bottom-up theorizing in the sociology of education. People apply Bourdieu's theory of 'Cultural Capital', originated in the context of France, to Indian situation. Since the theory originated in a context very different from India, there are limits to which the theory can be applied to India. This chapter tries to show, taking Bourdieu as a case, that substitution of class by caste is not enough to adapt western theories of the sociology of education into Indian situation. It tries to elaborate this by engaging with the issue of 'inclusion'—a major concern in the sociology of education in India. Inclusion has been construed as a function of external physical acts and processes. Academicians comment about the degree of exclusion in the acts and processes of the world outside university and sometimes in it. But while doing this, they forget that their very act of theorising can also be exclusionary when it doesn't incorporate the voice of the marginalised. This chapter reflects on the inclusivity of theorisation in the sociology of education in India in terms of incorporating caste.

Part II deals with one of the major consequences of the caste system in India—reservation policy. Some of the contested issues of reservation policy are: economic criteria as a basis of reservation, the issue of 'creamy layer' and reservation in the judiciary.

Chapter Seven deals with a popular polemic around reservation—'what will happen if everyone starts claiming reservation!' This is what the *Patel* agitation led by Hardik Patel demanded—'give reservation to us or abolish reservation altogether'. If one thinks impulsively then one might think that it's better to abolish reservation altogether. This sort of thinking can only happen when one is not clear about the justification for reservations. But if one is clear about the justifications for reservation of SC/ST then this need not be the conclusion. This essay, written in the wake of the *Patel* agitation, summarises some of the main justifications for reservation of SC/ST and counters some of the common objections to it. The stance taken in this essay is that 'exclusive economic criteria portrays as if government jobs are only about livelihood, not power'. This stance was later supported by Suhas Palshikar in *The Indian Express* who wrote, 'It is not a demand for social justice but proportional power-sharing that underlies the new quota agitations'.[1] It was also argued in the essay that economic criteria cannot take into account and compensate social discrimination. This stance was later supported by Satish Deshpande in *The Indian Express:*

> According to the alternate view, the essential purpose of reservation is not—and has never been—the redressal of poverty, "backwardness", or some other deficiency suffered by the lower castes. Reservation is the remedy for an upper-caste disease—namely, the practice of systematic caste discrimination legitimised for centuries by law and custom. It counters the socially coerced exclusion of lower castes from positions of power and privilege with constitutionally mandated inclusion via quotas.[2]

Chapter Eight deals with another polemic about reservation—the issue of the better off sections within a particular category taking away the benefits of reservation. This is the 'creamy layer' issue in legal jargon. When the issue of creamy layer is raised, SC/ST feel guilty. It is as if some well off SC/ST is stealing from some poor SC/ST! The issue of creamy layer raised by the upper castes projects them as some sort of benevolent white nights working for better implementation of reservation scheme than even the SC/ST themselves. But can it be possible that the upper castes can be more sympathetic to the SC/ST than the SC/ST themselves! The article dissects the creamy layer argument by pointing out that 'SC/ST belonging to creamy layer are still a sub-category of SC/ST. They do not become general category'. This argument finds support in an article in the *dailyO* where the author writes, 'However, there must be some safeguards. One, it must be ensured that these quotas are filled by these category people only and never go to a general category person'.[3]

Chapter Nine analyses a problematic judgement on the creamy layer—*Jarnail Singh v Lachhmi Narain Gupta* on 26 September, 2018. This judgement delivered a sort of double whammy. First it made creamy layer, which was always applicable to the OBC, applicable to the SC/ST. Second, it applied creamy layer at the stage of promotion jumping the gun in logic because so far creamy layer was applicable at the entry stage only. Ambedkar theorised that a class, when it follows endogamy, becomes a caste. But that happens over centuries! The court's contention that SC/ST IAS, after doing a few years of job, lose their class and caste. The court thinks that what happens over centuries can be achieved in a few years!

Chapter 10 deals with one of the theoretical gordian knots regarding reservation—the fifty per cent ceiling. The fifty per cent ceiling, laid down by the Supreme Court, works like a *Laxman rekha*. This creates a formidable difficulty for many states in accommodating various vociferous groups in reservation. The IXth Schedule is no solution as there is no logic or reality of the IXth Schedule's immunity from judicial review. It appears as if the fifty per cent ceiling is based on sound logic while actually it is not. The fifty per cent ceiling is actually on the basis of the principle of equality and not proportionality. If we apply the principle of proportionality, which is a balance between justice and efficiency, then the fifty per cent ceiling loses its sanctity.

Chapter 11 deals with yet another issue around reservation—what happens to the persons after they enter the system through reservation? Are they going to be judged by the same 'general yardstick' or is there a need for tweaking the yardstick for them? Instinctively we feel that the yardstick needs to be adjusted on the same ground on which it was adjusted at the entrance to the system first of all. This is the justification for reservation in promotion which has been existing for some time. However, a theoretical justification is required for non-applicability of the 'general yardstick' in a wholesale manner to persons after they enter the system through reservation. This was the theoretical issue in the expulsion of 73 students by IIT Roorkee in July 2015 and the subsequent decision to allow re-examination following the orders of the Uttarakhand High Court. Almost all of these students belonged to the reserved categories. It wasn't the case that these students were not given reservation. They got into IIT Roorkee by reservation but now they were evicted because of their low grade. The article, written in the wake of this issue, asked: 'Can one take away in the name of autonomy and merit what one gives in the name of social justice?' The dilemma has been articulated as 'giving with one hand and taking away with the other'. Such analogy was used by the Punjab & Haryana High Court while setting aside income-based sub category under the backward classes quota. It mentioned, 'The end result is that the State has given a benefit with one hand only to take it away with the other'.[4]

Such an issue has ramifications far beyond the ambit of education. If giving with one hand and taking away with the other is allowed, then virtually the entire reservation and affirmative action measures can effectively come to a halt because people can be evicted in the name of merit right after the moment they get into the system through reservation.

Instinctively we feel that such a thing could not have been the aim of the Constitution. This leads us to the question—what can be the implication and justification of affirmative action and reservation beyond the entrance? Does the definition of 'education' mean only the 'first year' or the 'total duration' of the course? Does the definition of a 'job' or 'service' mean only the entrance stage and nothing afterwards? Does access mean just being allowed through the 'gate' and not in the 'house'?

The next chapter deals with another contentious issue of reservation—reservation in judiciary. Normally reservation in the higher judiciary is attempted to be justified on the ground that the supreme court and high courts are very much part of the state and they are subject to the constitutional provisions of reservation. But the judiciary itself doesn't agree with this construction of higher judiciary as 'public employment'. But, could there be any jurisprudential justification for reservation in higher judiciary? Any justification for reservation in higher judiciary must penetrate the shield of 'independence of judiciary' in a liberal democracy. When others quarrel, they go to court. But who is to arbitrate when judges seem to disagree beyond a point? In sum, who is going to judge the judges! Roughly this translates into how to define judicial independence and the consequences thereof. This chapter employs some of the jurisprudential grounds to advocate for reservation in higher judiciary in India.

The last chapter in Part II deals with reservation in the private sector which is probably a theoretical gordian knot. While reservation in government employment can be justified on many grounds, justification for reservation in the private sector seems very difficult. It is not 'our' private sector the way it is 'our' government. While past discrimination and 'power-sharing' can be invoked for reservation in the government and the public sector, only present discrimination can be invoked for reservation in the private sector. However, the government style reservation cannot be implemented in the private sector, e.g. the OBC reservation. This article tries to solve the issue by taking a 'continuum' approach rather than a 'binary' approach employed in such discussions so far.

Part III deals with the interface between the criminal law and caste. The most prominent criminal law which is a 'special law' in India related to caste violence is SC/ST (Prevention of Atrocities) Act 1989. This is not only a criminal law but has many features which can be considered civil—for example the provision of compensation. Chapter 14 deals with one of the most unstudied aspects of this law—the 'false' cases. Accusation by upper castes of false cases by SC/ST using the Atrocities Act has been around for quite some time. However, the nomenclature 'false' case itself has been nothing less than mystical. The confusion prevails because the commonsensical notion of false case and the legal terminology 'false' case are two different phenomena. This chapter demystifies the legal category called 'false' by examining 100 false cases each under the SC/ST (Prevention of Atrocities) Act 1989 and Section 498A of the IPC.

Chapters 15 and 16 dissect the Supreme Court judgement *Subhash Kashinath Mahajan v State of Maharashtra* which introduced certain restrictions to the Atrocities Act making it practically toothless. The restriction introduced was that the police cannot arrest a person under this Act without first having a preliminary inquiry, submitted then to the senior superintendent of police (SSP), and then SSP permitting in writing. The only thing about the Atrocity Act that the upper castes fear is the prospect of immediate arrest because ensuring conviction of upper castes in the court has never been easy by the weak and poor SC/ST. Therefore, this restriction practically took away all the potency of the Atrocity Act. The court judgement was based on the NCRB data on 'false cases' under the Atrocities Act. Chapters 15 and 16 counter this judgement—one taking a jurisprudential route and another drawing from an empirical study on false cases from a state which has one of the highest rates of false cases in India. Chapter 15 shows that the statistics compared by the Supreme

Court is not comparable—for example 'Final Report' (false case) rate and 'conviction rate'. Final Report is a judgement by the police while conviction/acquittal is by the court. Chapter 16 drawing upon a study, examines whether the "final reports," which is the official term for closed cases under the Scheduled Castes and the Scheduled Tribes (Prevention of Atrocities) Act, 1989, are justified or not. The popularly accepted notion is that the act is misused by the members of the SC/ST against the upper castes, but there is no acknowledgement of its misuse by the upper castes using the former as proxy.

SC/ST are discriminated not only directly but also indirectly. Chapter 17 highlights the issue of 'indirect discrimination' in the context of universities. The protest after the suicide of Rohith Vemula gave rise to a demand for something called 'Rohit Act'. What would be the contours of the 'Rohit Act' was left undefined. While people could figure out that what had been happening in the university was discrimination, they were not able to give a suitable name to it because it was not looking like the usual discrimination. They were not able to give the name 'indirect discrimination' because there is not much discussion in India about indirect discrimination. How can we create just and non-discriminatory spaces in universities when the discriminatory practices are not obvious and apparent? The chapter suggests two ways—reporting and addressing indirect discrimination and a periodic 'discrimination audit' of educational institutions.

The last chapter probes the general theoretical linkage between caste exclusion and law in India. Can we think of something like 'inclusive law'? No, because it never strikes us. The law by definition is supposed to be inclusive. When other spheres like 'social' perpetrate exclusion, the law is supposed to come to the rescue of the SC/ST. But the trajectory of exclusion of the marginalised by law happens during the law's formation, its various manifestation in terms of general and special laws and its operation. Thus, exclusion by law is an issue that one has to be constantly vigilant. This essay attempts to elaborate this with reference to the Scheduled Castes and Scheduled Tribes in India.

NOTES

1. Suhas Palshikar, "The New Reservation", *The Indian Express*, August 1, 2018.
2. Satish Deshpande, "How Not to Review Reservations", *The Indian Express*, December 5, 2015.
3. Niranjan Kumar, "Why it's time to rethink India's reservation policy", dailyO, https://www.dailyo.in/politics/reservation-supreme-court-sc-st-obc-caste-narendra-modi-bjp/story/1/26200.html Accessed on August 22, 2018.
4. Apoorva Mandhani, "Punjab & Haryana HC Sets Aside Income-Based Sub Category Under Backward Classes Quota", live Law.in. https://www.livelaw.in/punjab-haryana-hc-sets-aside-income-based-sub-category-under-backward-classes-quota-read-order/ Accessed on August 9, 2018.

PART I
CASTE

2

Shastra (scripture) or *Shastra* (power) Origin of Caste: Sociological Imaginations

When we have complete information like census, we don't need any theorisation. But when the information is incomplete then we approach it with some theorisation. We can try to figure out the origin of caste by applying sociological imaginations. That both power and ideology is necessary to maintain a system is almost common sense. However, determining the primacy of one of these two is not easy. The debate around Louis Dumont's *Homo Hierarchicus* (1970) maintains that the idea of purity-impurity and the ideology around it maintains the caste system. An evolutionary theory of origin of caste can be built around this by saying that people gradually subscribed to various *shastras* over 2,000 years and that's how the caste system came to where it is now. In contrast to this, the alternative theory could be that force is what maintains the system and could have been responsible for the origin of the system. Partap Aggarwal substantiates such a proposition in his empirical study in one village in Rajasthan:

> In other words, the greater the gain or loss in power of a caste, the more the change in the religious behaviour of its members. The result has created uniformity among the castes. Clearly, power and not religion maintains caste hierarchy. I must further point out that the pollution line which separates the untouchables castes from the clean castes is, at least in *Chavandi Kalan*, not nearly as uncrossable as it has been claimed to be in Orissa (Bailey 1957)

> and in South India by other researchers. I may suggest that the reason why the pollution line was so easily crossed in *Chavandi Kalan* was that the amount of land and political power gained by the *Chamar*s was significantly large (Aggarwal 1969, 551).

However, the 'ideology' theory rather than the force/ power theory is preponderant in the discussion on caste in universities. Why is this so? Gerald D. Berreman explains:

> As noted above, India is frequently cited as an example of a society in which people of deprived and subject status are content with their lot, primarily justifying it by religion and philosophy. This is the characteristic of caste in India most often cited to distinguish it from hereditary systems elsewhere, notably in the southern United States. On the basis of my research and the literature, I maintain that this is not accurate and therefore not a valid distinction. Its prevalence is attributable in part, at least, to the vested interests of the advantaged and more articulate castes in the perpetuation of the caste system and the maintenance of a favorable view of it to outsiders. The same arguments and the same biases are frequently presented by apologists for the caste system of the southern United States (Berreman 1960, 124).

The claim that the system was accepted voluntarily by the lower castes is like saying that the Diwani rights given by Mughal emperor Shah Alam II, to Robert Clive were voluntary and the 'subsidiary alliance' entered into by the Indian princes with the British was voluntary.

The voluntaristic theory of caste looks like Functionalism or the Social Contract theory and the criticisms about these latter two can be directed at the voluntaristic theory of caste. It is like saying that the constitution originates in contract and is maintained by contract. Pierre Bourdieu calls the 'social contract' as the 'origin myth' of liberal democracy. Similarly, the theory that the lower castes voluntarily accepted the *shastra*s and the supremacy of the *Brahman* is the origin myth of the caste system which actually might have originated and maintained by force.

However, even if we accept the power theory, we need to

build an evolutionary account to suit the power theory just like there is the *shastric* tale to suit the ideological account. The building of an evolutionary account will involve the interaction of history and sociology. Hamilton and Walton (1988) point out that although we are accustomed to think that new sociology uses old history as evidence, the reverse is possible and inviting as a method for historical sociology. This means sometimes we can employ sociology to unravel history.

A good example of applying sociological imagination to something historical or mythological, could be a westerner's nonchalance to Lord Sri Ram's exile to the forest for 14 years. When Shri Ram was condemned to 14 years exile in the forest by Dashrath, there was wailing all over Ayodhya. But the westerner may wonder what's the big deal about it. His reasoning can go like this. If we go back in history then the spread of jungle will gradually increase and therefore by the time of Ram, which could be thousands of years back, there could be jungle all around Ayodhya. Therefore, going to forest would have meant just going to the outskirt of the city. So, what is the big deal! This imagination is possible only for a westerner because his thinking is not circumscribed by the Indian beliefs. Our deeply ingrained Hindu belief will simply not allow us to think beyond what is told to us. This is how a sociological imagination can be applied to history. The origin of caste, which could have happened more than 2,000 years back, and about which we don't have much material sources, can be fruitfully inquired into by applying some sociological imagination.

Origin of caste by force—direct involvement of *Brahmans* in ruling

The origin of caste by force can be constructed in the following way. Initially a particular group of people became victorious. Evidence of use of horse and iron is absent in the Indus Valley Civilisation while they are mentioned in *Rigveda*. This could be the reason of *Aryan* victory over the native population. Then differentiation arose. It may be the case that the *Brahmans* might have been the most powerful within the *Arya varna.* Ambedkar has listed the fights between the *Brahmana* and *Kshatriya* which can be constructed as power struggle within the *Arya varna*. The transition of *varna* classification in the following way can be interpreted as this struggle:

- *Arya varna* and *dasa varna* (early *Rigveda* 1,500 C. B.C.)
- *Brahman, Rajanya* and *Vis* (later *Rigveda*)
- *Brahman, Kshatriya, Vaisya* and *shudra* (*pururshashukta* in *Rigveda)*
- *Manusmriti* (3rd C. A.D.)—mention of myriad castes and *bahya* (outside the fold)

The question arises how political power transformed into the caste system? Transposing sociology into history, the following account can be constructed. The powerful/smart within the *Arya varna* (the *Brahman)* built all customary/legal privileges. In this case it was more systematic than the shamans, other rituals, and superstitions regarding power and privilege which exist till today. To point out some similarity elsewhere, the selling of 'indulgence' in medieval Europe was like *prayaschit.* The powerful structure the system in such a way that they appropriate material and symbolic privileges. It was the right of the *Brahmans* to receive gift and imperative of others to give gift. From the 6th century onwards they got land grants that was absolved from tax, interference from king's soldiers, and along with the land grant came the population inhabiting the land. Lower groups emulated the upper (powerful) strata as happens always. That's how the social practice crystallised over the hundreds of years and gave rise to caste. With regard to emulation, M.N. Srinivas mentioned 'westernisation' which basically means that the elite in India emulated the west and were not simply satisfied with their already elite *Brahman* status.

If force was the basis, then *Brahmans* must have been the original muscle men. We must not forget that *Brahmans* were originally in charge of the sacrificial violence. The myth of Dronacharya, Parsuraman is to underscore the military credential of *Brahmans*. But, then why *Kshatriya* was assigned to rule? The explanation could be that the ruling involves hard work which the *Brahmans* did not assign to themselves theoretically. But practically they have done enough ruling as well without which the ritual hierarchy could not have sustained over the ages.[1] While Mahajan (1970) shows the *Brahmans* ruling dynasties in ancient times, others show their involvement in ruling even under the British. The following list illustrates this chronologically:

- *Sunga* and *Kanva* dynasty after the fall of *Mauryas*
- The *Hindushahi* dynasty of Kabul (9th century) when Mahammad bin Kasim invaded
- Lalitaditya Muktapida was the *Brahman* emperor of Kashmir from 724 to 760 A.D. under the *Karkota* dynasty
- *Vakataka* dynasty—Vidhyashakti, founder of Vakataka dynasty was supposed to be a *Dvija* (cave XVI inscription of Ajanta). They had marriage alliance with the Guptas who were *vaishya*.
- *Kadamba* dynasty—The founder changed his name from Mayura *sharman* to Mayura *varman* to emphasize his change from a *Brahman* to a *Kshatriya*
- *Pallava* were supposed to be *brahman-kshatriya*
- The interpretation around *kandalur salai*—one interpretation is that it is not *pandya* territory but hereditary military academy run by *Brahmans*. The fall of this paved the way for the rise of *Chola* (Veluthat, 1993).
- The *Sena* dynasty that ruled from Bengal through the 11th and 12th centuries were called *Brahma-Kshatriyas*
- The *Peshwa* of Pune
- Madanna and Akkanna were two *Brahman* brothers who rose to prominence in the sultanate of Golkonda between 1674 and 1685 A.D. (Kruijtzer 2002).
- Of the 125,000 native soldiers in the Bengal army,

nearly 100,000 were Brahman (Rao 2019, 89)

- '...according to the Maddox Settlement Report, which covered the third district of coastal Orissa, Balasore, the *Brahmans* and the *Karans* together made up slightly less than half of the landowners, both during 1836-45 and 1890-1900'. (Lerche 1993, 257)
- Civil service during the British—it was the over-representation of *Brahmans* in the civil service that gave rise to the backward class movement in south India.

One can see that the direct involvement of *Brahmans* in ruling continues from ancient period to British and then post-independence India. The example of Madanna and Akkanna shows that even during Muslim rule they did not go into oblivion. Both the Muslim and British involved them in administration. Kruijtzer (2002) mentions that During 17th century the word *Brahman* became synonymous with financial administrating and book keeping. Records of the East India Company mention *Brahman* of so and so. This could not have been possible if they did not have the necessary experience in the previous ages.

Did the king genuinely accept the superiority of the *Brahman*?

Once we accept the force theory, we need to explain why the king showed reverence to the *Brahman*. There were a number of dynasties like Samudragupta, Satavahan, who were not *Brahman* but performed *Asvamedh, Rajsuya* etc. which reflect their adherence to the *Brahmanic* ideology. Why did they do so? Analysing this involves accepting the proposition that the *Brahman* (*rajpurohit*) was number one in status both de jure and de facto. If this proposition fails then the argument that the *Brahman* was number one even without being the ruler fails.

If we speculate about the ancient period, could the seat of the *rajpurohit* be at a higher pedestal than the king! 'Although *Brahmans* were indexed at the top of the ritual order of things, when honours were given in temple festivals throughout the state, they were given first to the kings and only afterward to the *Brahman* (Dirks 2001, 69). Translated to the contemporary times, while the government on paper is run by the President, actually the Prime Minister runs the government and Prime Minister is the real seat of power. The President remains the President so long he does not oppose the Prime Minister. The moment he or she opposes the Prime Minister obviously s/he will face the hurdles. Ambedkar would opine that that sort of person does not become the President first of all.

If the *Brahman* could put himself at the top of the hierarchy by holding power, then the reverse is that he suffers when without power. If we exercise our imagination, we can figure this out. Historically, there have been innumerable cases of razing of temples against which the *Brahmans* could do very little. The Jagannath temple of Puri was vandalised many times by the Muslim rulers of Bengal. In fact, once they vandalised it so thoroughly that a saving notion was created that the statue was taken to an island in Chilika lake by the *Brahmans* before the vandalisation and thus was not vandalised. Earlier, while soldiers were conquering, depredation ensued. Could the marauding soldiers have spared the *Brahmans*?

Second, if we assume stratification within a stratum, then, there could not have been any comparison between the *raja* and the *rajpurohit* vis-á-vis the ordinary soldier and the *Brahman*. The *Brahman* might not have approved his daughter to be married to a royal family (*Kshatriya*) because the *Kshatriya* is inferior in status. But could a princess have agreed to marry a *Brahman?* A humble *Brahman* may not even get an audience before the king. As a reverse of it, if the *Brahman* would have insisted on being treated as superior to the king then he probably would have been shown his place. In the present times in an educational institute there are the faculty, and trustees as in a temple. Who is higher in the hierarchy? Though the faculty position is number one in academic matters the faculty is appointed by the governing board (trustees).

Theoretically it was the *Brahman* who should have

decided the caste matters as he is the interpreter of *dharma.* But even the British, in the manner of earlier *rajas*, decided caste matters, the most famous being the census of 1931. Dirks (2001) mentions that the *Kallars* of Puddukkotai sided with the British in the Poligar wars and retained their princely status while elsewhere they were branded as criminals and had a caste status of untouchable. The same was with the *Maravars.* All these examples throw doubt about a general de facto number one status of *Brahman* without power. But, as of now, we have a picture of general *Brahman* superiority. How has it happened?

Dirks (2001) and many scholars have pointed out that this happened especially during the colonial period when *Brahmans* were entrusted to bring out authoritative texts on Hinduism and they used this opportunity to portray *Manusmriti* as the *Dharmashastra* par excellence which is accepted by all. Thus, the notion—that *Brahman* as the superior of all is accepted by all—was constructed. The coincidence of collaboration between Orientalists, *Brahman* pundits and the ethnographic necessities (need to know the land for revenue purpose) led to the establishing of the authority of the *Dharmashastras.* 'Whatever its historical status, however, most scholars today agree that it (*Manusmriti)* took on unprecedented status as an "applied" legal document only under early British rule' (Dirks 2001, 34). The rise of men of pen in Hindustan is generally in the 18th century (Chris Bayly cited in Dirks 2001). Flavia Agnes (2001) points out that during the colonial period local traditions, more liberal to women, were undermined and a *Brahman*-patriarchal law about women was instituted.

Even if we settle the status issue between the king and the *Brahman,* we still need to explain the reverence, the donation to *Brahman* by most castes in non-ideological terms. P. Chidambaram, a former finance and home minister articulates in this way: 'Why did the *Kshatriyas* and *Vaishyas,* who had power and money, accept the *Brahman* as their superior?' The usual interpretation is that the *Brahmanical* values hold sway in their mind. But this cannot be the only interpretation. There can be other interpretations as well. It can be looked at as 'conspicuous consumption' (a term coined by Thorstein Veblen). Sometimes the powerful display reverence for the powerless. But this cannot be construed as genuine reverence but rather some sort of conspicuous consumption. Public servants are more rulers of the public than servants. Teachers are revered on special days as guru in India by the politicians but on other days they are even beaten mercilessly when they agitate for their pay. There is no problem of the powerful showing symbolic reverence, sympathy etc. for the powerless but it is a different case when the powerless demands some sort of material equivalent of the reverence that can't obviously be given. The land and the gold given to the *Brahman* was substantial for the *Brahman* but would have constituted a small part of the total wealth of the *shudra* king.

Why did not the *shudra* king demolish the system?

Mahapadmananda, Shivaji are examples of *shudra* kings. Could they have abolished the caste system? But another question could be that why would they undertake a very difficult task not necessary for them? We must remember that caste is not a one man show. It is a systemic show. Therefore, the *shudra* king's ability to demolish caste system is unrealistic because one king does not make the entire community empowered. The formidable Akbar tried to create *din-i-ilahi* but could gather only a few followers. Sometime back Sonia Gandhi was the most powerful person in India which did not mean that women were powerful in India.

Once you are on top of the system by conquering the system it makes sense to use the system to your advantage rather than abolish the very system and start building a new system afresh. This is what Shivaji did. After consolidating himself with a liberal dose of service of Muslims under him he got Gaga Bhatt to consecrate him rather than creating a new hierarchy (Vajpeyi 2010). One interpretation could be that he is submitting to the system. But another could be that he has successfully tamed the system. Similarly, the pragmatic Akbar had marriage relation with the equally pragmatic *rajputs* and did not press forth his new religion.

Once you are on the top of the system you have nothing to fear from the system. The *Brahman* has nothing to fear from the caste system and therefore they would not like to abolish the system. The question only remains of the OBC and SC/ST. One of the rare instances when somebody came to the top of the system and yet abolished the system was J. Krishnamurthy who abolished the very 'Order of The Star' of which he was the chosen head.

If the theoretical supremacy of the *Brahman* was not a practical problem to the *shudra* king then why the *Brahman* was never pulled down from his high pedestal theoretically as well? It's not easy. If the *Brahmans* were to be pulled down then one had to create an alternate framework. If caste goes, then class can come and if that goes then *nomenclatura* can come which was the stratification device in erstwhile Soviet Russia. If the naxals become victorious they will create an alternate framework. On the other hand, there are those who try to achieve power within the Indian constitutional framework. If the King were to declare that he was superior to *Brahman* he had to create an alternate framework. The *Brahman* was anyway no obstacle to what he wanted. The donation to *Brahman* was part of prestige/conspicuous consumption/ piety plus legitimacy build up. A king would have never liked to be seen as merely a robber/usurper.

Conclusion

The notion of *shastra* (scripture) upholding the caste system can be a very good diversion tactic. The *shastra* (scripture) was always buttressed by *shastra* (power). Status comparison between *Brahman* and *Kshatriya* should not be stretched too far because both, coming from the same stock of *Arya varna*, were directly involved in ruling in a sort of coalition government. A king tracing his origin as *brahma-kshatriya* symbolises a truce and a pact about joint ruling. There is perennial disgruntle in a coalition government. But that does not lead always to the fall of the government. The more we recognise the power principle the better we are equipped to deal with caste.

NOTE

1. See Chapter 2 "History of Brahmans and Military: A Long-Term Analysis from The Vedas". Chuyen, pp. 63-92.

REFERENCES

Aggarwal, Partap C., 'Changing Religious Practices-Their Relationship to Secular Power in a Rajasthan Village'. *Economic and Political Weekly* 4, No. 12 (1969): 547-551.

Agnes, Flavia, *Law and Gender Inequality: The Politics of Women's Rights in India*. New Delhi: Oxford, 2001.

Berreman, Gerald D., 'Caste in India and the United States'. *American Journal of Sociology* 66, No. 2 (1960): 120-127.

Dirks, Nicholas B., Castes *of Mind: Colonialism and the Making of Modern India*. Delhi: Permanent Black, 2004.

Chuyen, Gilles, *Who is A Brahman? The Politics of Identity in India*. New Delhi: Manohar, Centre De Sciences Humaines, 2004.

Dumont, L., *Homo Hierarchicus: The Caste System & Its Implications*. Delhi: Oxford University Press, 1970.

Hamilton, Gary H., John Walton, 'History in Sociology'. *The Future of Sociology* edited by Edgar Borgatta, Karen S. Cook. Newbury Park, California: Sage Publications, 1988, pp. 181-199.

Kruijtzer, Gijs, 'Madanna, Akkanna and the *Brahman* Revolution: A Study of Mentality, Group Behaviour and Personality in Seventeenth-Century India'. *Journal of the Economic and Social History of the Orient* 45, No. 2 (2002): 231-267.

Lerche, Jens, 'Dominant Castes, Rajas, *Brahmans* and Inter-Caste Exchange Relations in Coastal Orissa: Behind the Facade of the 'Jajmani System'. *Contributions to Indian Sociology* 27, No. 2 (1993): 237–266.

Mahajan, V.D., *Ancient India*. Delhi: S. Chand & Co., 1970.

Rao, Parimala V., 'Colonial State as 'New Manu'? Explorations in Education Policies in Relation to Dalit and Low-Caste Education in the Nineteenth-Century India'. *Contemporary Education*

Dialogue 16, No. 1 (2019): 84-107.

Vajpeyi, Ananya, 'Śūdradharma and Legal Treatments of Caste'. *Hinduism and Law: An Introduction* edited by Timothy Lubin, Donald R. Davis Jr., Jayanth K. Krishnan. New York: Cambridge University Press, 2010, pp. 154-166.

Veluthat, Kesavan, *Political Structure of Early Medieval South India*. London: Sangam Books Limited, 1993.

3

Amartya Sen, Capability Approach and Caste[1]

A discussion on caste is inextricably a discussion on social justice. Amartya Sen's various writings have focussed on the capability approach and he has specifically used this approach in one of his books *The Idea of Justice* (2010). He prefers a comparative approach to that of a transcendental institutional approach to justice. Justice should be a comprehensive outcome and not just a culmination outcome. Therefore, mere *niti* (principles, procedures) is not sufficient for justice but what is required is *nyaya* (comprehensive outcome). This can be attained by taking a comparative rather than a transcendental approach by 'public reasoning' and taking recourse to 'partial ordering' rather than waiting for the 'complete ordering'. Thus, capability approach (focussing on individual as well as groups) with its focus on substantive opportunity is better suited than transcendental institutional approach as a guide in the matter of justice.

The present chapter has the following sections: (1) Cognizance of caste as an unjust institution. (2) Countering blatant injustice (untouchability) does not require sophisticated theorisation. (3) Justice delayed is justice denied—Preference of a comparative-actual behavioural approach to that of a transcendental-institutional approach (4) The focus on actual behaviour—Contract/Utilitarianism vs asymmetry of power/imperfect obligation (5) The Goal of Justice—Formal vs substantive; *Niti*-procedure-culmination outcome vs *nyaya*-

realization-comprehensive outcome (6) The procedure to achieve the goal—'Veil of ignorance' vs Impartial spectator, open impartiality, public reason (7) Capability as the 'valid justice tender'(8) Critique.

(1) Cognizance of caste as an unjust institution

Sen takes cognizance of caste as an unjust social institution. However, there is a transition in the weight he chooses to give to caste. Caste has never become a chapter in any of his books unlike gender. While he has taken his honest cognizance of caste in his book in 1995, *India: Economic Development and Social Opportunity* (co-authored with Jean Dreze), his book in 2010, *The Idea of Justice,* is almost silent on caste compared to gender, poverty, health and education. It is as if caste loses its visibility when one is writing about the world at large. While social issues of poverty, health and education have been his perennial concern, it is only gender as a major social stratification that engages his attention. Sen makes the following observations about caste in the book *India: Economic Development and Social Opportunity*:

- Missing woman—how the process of *sanskritisation* has resulted in lower castes changing their attitude to women. This has resulted in their devaluing women resulting in lower survival of girl children;
- How Kerala's progress was contributed to by its anti-upper caste movement;
- How lower castes can improve themselves through public political action.

His straightforward cognizance of caste as an oppressive social institution is evident from the following passage in the book:

> 'in large parts of the country, local governance is in the hands of upper-caste men from privileged classes, who are only weakly accountable to the community and often end up using local public services as instruments of patronage. In some cases, the rural elite has been known not only to be indifferent to the

> general promotion of local public services but even to *obstruct* their expansion, to prevent the empowerment of disadvantaged groups. In Uttar Pradesh, for instance, it is still possible to find villages where a powerful landlord has actively opposed the creation of a village school' (Dreze & Sen 1995, 107).

However, this was not his solo opinion. This was the joint opinion of Amartya Sen and Jean Dreze. In his solo opinion Sen is rather evasive about caste evidenced from the following excerpts from *The Idea of Justice*:

> 'We identify with people of the same religion, same language group, same race, same gender, same political beliefs or same profession (2010, 129).

> 'however, since injustices relate, often enough, to hardy social divisions, linked with divisions of class, gender, rank, location, religion, community and other established barriers... (ibid, 389).

It looks like as if he does not want to hurt his upper caste admirers. His evasiveness about caste is indirectly evident in his reading of Indian history. Unlike Ambedkar who was not enamoured by the glory of ancient India, Sen projects a glorious historical India. Sen projects Ashoka as a very benevolent and enlightened saint king but does not comment on the facts that: 1. Ashoka did not return the independence to the people of Kalinga; 2. did not completely waive the tax on people of Kalinga but reduced only to one eighth; 3. threatened the tribals of the frontier to behave. It seems that it is quite difficult for him to say things negative about Indian history. In *The Idea of Justice*, Sen says that 'I have heard that Manu is a fascist lawgiver' (2010, 20; footnote). He is choosing not to say it himself but says 'I have heard'. Could not he decide himself whether Manu was a fascist lawgiver or not! Then he gives some examples of positive statements from Manu like—'where women are not revered, all rights are fruitless'. Generally, Manu is considered oppressive, especially to women and lower castes. I do not think that there will be too many examples of humane statements in *Manusmriti*.

Justice will indeed collapse if a few positive statements/acts override a plethora of negative acts/statements. Sen also gives the example of the notion of *mastyanyaya* in the sense that one should be satisfied with whatever one can do rather than waiting for the ultimate justice (so that one avoids *mastyanyaya*). This is evident from his general support for partial ordering. However, ancient lawgivers of India have used the analogy of *mastyanyaya* to justify the rule of a king and *varnashramdharma*. The big fish eats small fish in the world of *mastyanyaya*, but there is freedom as well. Marx opined, in a positive sense, that the labor became free for the first time in capitalism; of course, to live or to die. But freedom per se is not a bad idea in contrast to a golden cage. Thus, Sen reads the history of India in a particular way that will be in stark contrast to Ambedkar. Similarly, unlike a Dalit, it is not easy for him to miss anything positive in the Indian tradition. In the book *The Argumentative Indian* he mentions:

> In the Indian epic Mahabharata, dating from around two thousand years ago, Bharadvaja, an argumentative interlocutor, responds to the defense of the caste system by Bhrigu (a pillar of the establishment) by asking: "We all seem to be affected by desire, anger, fear, sorrow, worry, hunger, and labor; how do we have caste differences then? (2005, 11).

But a seasoned academician that he is, he also writes a little later:

> It would be just as much of a mistake to treat the argumentative tradition as being of no relevance whatever to contemporary Indian society as it would be to regard that tradition as powerfully effective on its own, irrespective of arrangements for politics, particularly of democratic politics (ibid, 38).

All these however do not point out that his theory can not be fruitfully applied to the analysis of caste. In the following I will rope him in discussion on caste.

(2) Countering blatant injustice (untouchability) does not require sophisticated theorisation.

This is the welcome starting point in Sen's scheme of justice. Research methodology employs the concept of 'face validity'. Law employs the notion of 'prima facie'. The notion of 'prima facie' assumes that it does not require a great deal of intelligence to spot gross injustice. This is a welcome counter to any post-modern notion of justice. It is also a necessary ingredient to Sen's schema of justice as Sen does not believe in a transcendental approach to justice. Though Sen does not mention caste much, his general position seems to be that gross injustice, evident from the face of it, does not need to wait for sophisticated theorization, to be removed. The gross and blatant injustice in the caste system is untouchability and atrocities. He mentions in his book *The Idea of Justice*:

> 'for the emergence of a shared and useful understanding of many substantive issues of rights and duties (and also of rights and wrongs) there is no need to insist that we must have agreed complete orderings or universally accepted full partitions of the just, strictly separated from the unjust; for example, a common resolve to fight for the abolition of famines, or genocide, or terrorism, or slavery, or untouchability, or illiteracy, or epidemics etc. does not require that there be a similarly extensive agreements on the appropriate formula for inheritance rights, or income tax schedules, or levels of minimum wages, or copyright laws. The basic relevance of the distinct perspectives—some congruent, some divergent—of the people of the world (diversely diverse as we human beings are) is part of the understanding that open impartiality tends to generate. There is nothing defeatist in this recognition' (2010, 145).

Justice need not wait for complete ordering but can move on the basis of partial ordering. Upper caste chauvinists try to drag lower castes into the theoretical vortex of economic criteria of reservation and caste versus the race. We need not suspend action till we settle the debate on the best criteria for reservation or whether caste is race or not.

(3) Justice delayed is justice denied—Preference of a comparative-actual behavioural approach to that of a transcendental-institutional approach

Caste as a form of injustice is a legitimate subject of a theory of justice. *The Idea of Justice* (2010) is Sen's elaborate view on justice. Sen draws on his all earlier insights for his theory of justice in this book. Sen's point of departure is John Rawls. He calls Rawls's approach as 'transcendental institutional' in the tradition of a contractarian approach going back to Hobbes. While Rawlsian approach firmly underscores equality as integrally linked to the idea of 'justice', it is not useful pragmatically because of its 'transcendental institutional' approach. Sen prefers a comparative approach, closure to the reality than a transcendental approach of Rawls which uses a 'veil of ignorance'. He seems to say that 'justice delayed is justice denied'. He gives the metaphor of the Buridan's ass which died for not being able to decide the better hay stalk out of two. In support of actual behaviour in contrast to a transcendental just institution, Sen says:

> demanding more from behaviour today than could be expected to be fulfilled would not be a good way of advancing the cause of justice. This basic realisation must play a part in the way we think about justice and injustice today, and it will figure in the constructive work that follows in the rest of the book (ibid, 81).

The usefulness of focussing on institution is that it brings out how unjust caste as an institution is. According to Hindu religious texts caste is a transcendental institution based on the notion of *karma*. Even temporally speaking, caste seems to be a transcendental institution considering its long existence for thousands of years compared to race. But the focus on actual behaviour is also important because of the survival of caste against all other modern institutions including in foreign places. People's behaviour in India has not changed though we have created many institutions after independence that were supposed to go against caste. The putative establishment in India of the Anglo-Saxon notion of 'rule of law' through the constitution is an example. It is this mismatch between institution and behaviour that Sen is pointing out. He says that if the subscription to the contract is perfect then Rawls does not need a 'difference principle'.

Comparative approach is useful in the context of the current controversy related to comparison between caste and race. Sen gives the example of 'feminist' as an identity uncircumscribed by national borders. Similarly, caste and race can identify each other from a comparative viewpoint. It is not *Manusmriti* which enforces the prohibition of inter-caste marriage but the upper caste people who do it—internally through their belief and externally by employing force. Similarly, it is through belief and external force that racial inequality is buttressed. Just like the textual prohibition of inter caste marriage does not mean there is no inter-caste marriage, similarly there is no frequent inter-racial marriage without any textual prohibition.

(4) The focus on actual behaviour—Contract/Utilitarianism vs asymmetry of power/imperfect obligation

Once we choose to focus on actual behaviour, we are confronted with our assumptions of human behaviour. Self-seeking utilitarianism will result in a hypothetical social contract for the purpose of justice. However, if we can show that self-seeking is not an intrinsic propensity of humans, then we do not need a hypothetical contract for social justice. Actual behaviour will do.

> Even though [the] so called 'rational-choice theory' takes the rationality of choice to be characterized by intelligent pursuit of self-interest, it need not rule out the possibility that a person may have sympathy or antipathy towards others (Sen 2010, 188).

Sen's predominant criticism towards utilitarianism and rational choice rests on the premise that individuals may well be guided by others' wellbeing than theirs. But one has to apply the corollary of this premise to the caste system. We can be happy by making others happy but there can also be people who will be happy by making others unhappy e.g. in a revenge situation. The upper castes are unilaterally hostile to the lower castes. Caste does not follow a contractarian reasoning of mutual benefit or mutual hostility. It follows unilateral cooperation or unilateral hostility. Lower castes are supposed to serve the upper castes without any return as it is supposed to be their *dharma*. The prescription is unilateral and transcendental.

Contractarian reasoning becomes problematic especially in an asymmetric power situation like caste. Sen proposes the concept of 'imperfect obligation' of Kant as a remedy. In the section 'power and its obligation' in the *The Idea of Justice* Sen advocates that those who have more power in an asymmetric power situation have the unilateral obligation to think about the wellbeing of others who do not have such power. Somebody who has a reasonable circumstance to help others, even if he is not responsible for that misery, has an 'imperfect obligation' to help. Sen gives the example of the law in France which considers criminal omission as the omission to help those in trouble nearby in spite of one being capable of doing so. So, it is not the case that 'imperfect obligation' does not exist in the legal world. This perspective is indeed useful for the Atrocities Act. Presently the upper caste bystanders, who have effective power to intervene when atrocity happens, do not attract any criminal omission.

(5) The goal of justice—formal vs substantive;

Niti/procedure/culmination outcome *vs nyaya*/realisation/ comprehensive outcome

Sen distinguishes between two conceptions of justice. The institutional approach, which can be transcendental, has its goal the just institutions, leaving the outcomes at the hand of these just institutions. Such outcomes are mere 'culmination outcomes' which may be very different from what the just institutions aimed for. The other conception of justice, to which Sen subscribes, is process inclusive 'comprehensive outcome'. 'Comprehensive outcome' will not stop just at the 'just institutions' but will look into the outcomes.

The concept of comprehensive outcome can throw some light on reservation in the private sector. Presently, the private sector takes responsibility only for the fair procedure, but does not take any responsibility on whether these procedures are resulting in the desired outcome. Justice in the private sector is only the *niti*/procedure focussed but not the *nyaya*/ comprehensive outcome. There is liberty but not much bothering about the result. Comprehensive outcome will support the legal notion of 'proof by statistics' which exists in the legal system of European Union. Thus, if there is exceptionally small number of a certain category of people in an organisation, the onus is on the organisation to prove that its procedures are fair. The organisation can do this by showing that there is link between procedure to select and the job requirement. It cannot escape by citing some inane examination that has no link to the job requirement.

Comprehensive outcome also justifies the various measures against caste injustice. Untouchability in India was first abolished by the constitution. Later the Protection of Civil Rights Act 1955 repealed many state laws banning untouchability. Later again SC/ST (Prevention of Atrocities) Act was instituted in 1989. Comprehensive outcome has to continuously look at the institution whether they are delivering the result.

> we do, of course, choose between different 'game forms' here, but the choice of game forms is guided by their effectiveness in bringing about the social realization that is aimed at for the sake of liberty (Sen 2010, 316).

(6) The procedure to achieve the goal—'Veil of ignorance' vs Impartial spectator, public reason

Rawls used the hypothetical device of 'veil of ignorance' for impartiality. However, this won't help if we choose to focus on actual behaviour. In the real world, people do deviate from the contract they enter into. We are confronted with cultural relativism, in the matter of justice, if we focus on actual behaviour. What is justice for one, is injustice for another. Sen proposes two solutions for this impasse—the analogy of the 'impartial spectator' of Adam Smith and public reasoning. The impartial spectator is the voice from near and far and not only the members of the contractarian group. The usefulness of this device is that it takes care of:

1. enlightenment relevance in addition to membership entitlement.
2. Takes care of the concerns of non-contractarian members who are affected by the decision of the contractarian members.

Drawing from the first implication, non-Indian scholars' comment on caste is very necessary for a balanced view of caste. Louis Dumont will be a relevant case. Drawing from the second implication, upper caste scholars' theorisation of caste has to be moderated by *Dalit* scholars' theorisation. Lower castes are affected by upper caste scholars' theorisation. Ghurye defining tribal as 'backward Hindu' is a case in point. Many upper caste scholars valorising class at the expense of caste is another case. When confronted with such charges, the upper caste scholars often take resort to the shield of 'objectivity' and 'impartiality'. However, Sen advocates for 'open impartiality' and 'transpositional objectivity' guided by 'positional illumination'. One's position can create illusion but it can create illumination as well.

> 'in that framework, there would therefore be something of a lacuna in thinking of ethical objectivity only in terms of 'the view from nowhere', rather than 'from a delineated somewhere'. There can be special relevance in positional features that a capacious ethics must adequately acknowledge and appropriately take into account' (2010, 160).

Many upper caste scholars on caste do not mention their 'delineated somewhere' and project as if they are writing from 'the view from nowhere'. The attempt is to suppress the positional illusion. The antidote to positional illusion is public reason. The caste system may very well be rational to some but this can be subjected to public reasoning.

> 'the principal point that Mary Wollstonescraft is making here, as she does elsewhere, is that it is unsustainable to have a defence of the freedom of human beings that separates some people whose liberties matter from others not to be included in that favoured category' (Ibid, 116)... 'Wollstonecraft's argument has a huge reach, applying, for example to the status of untouchables in India' (Ibid, 116).

(7) Materials of justice—Capability as the valid justice tender

Sen gives a lot of importance to capability. His position is that instead of either 'resources' or 'liberty' capability should be the 'materials of justice'. Equality of liberty or resources (Rawlsian primary goods) does not take care of the desired outcome because of some of the intervening phenomena like physical disability. Physically disabled are worse off even with equal amount of primary goods. Sen mentions four different sources of conversion variance of income into capability

1. personal heterogeneity
2. diversities in the physical environment
3. Variations in social climate
4. Differences in relational perspective (Ibid, 255).

The intervening variables of 'social climate' and 'relational perspective' have important bearings on caste. Sen says regarding social climate, 'aside from public facilities, the nature of community relationships can be very important, as the recent literature on "social capital" has tended to emphasize'. 'Community relationship', the heart of social justice, is oppressive in caste. Economic betterment of lower castes automatically does not result in an egalitarian community relationship for them. In extreme cases, they may be denied housing even if they have the means to pay. In the section on 'disability, resources and capability' in *The Idea of Justice* Sen has discussed only physical disability but not social disability.

However, if we take into account social disability, then we can see how it is a huge hindrance in converting income into capability. What Sen calls as 'relational perspective' too has a pertinent bearing on caste. Sen cites the example given by Adam Smith 'to appear in public without shame' as a relational perspective. It means that more income is required in a rich neighbourhood 'to appear in public without shame'. While all that is required in a class system is more money 'to appear in public without shame', the challenge in the caste system is that no matter what's the income of a lower caste, can s/he appear in public without shame! An upper caste judge applied *gangajal* (holy water) to clean his desk which was earlier occupied by a lower caste judge. Caste is the most insurmountable among the ascription-based stratification. If a female becomes a male through surgery, the person will get a male status or will at least lose the female status. The offspring of an inter-racial marriage will get at least an intermediary status. But Manu condemns the offspring of an inter-caste marriage lower than the lowest between the couple. The Supreme Court has decided for the purpose of reservation that children will assume the caste of their father. However, it violates our commonsense that children of *Brahman* father and Dalit mother will be considered as *Brahman*. It is one thing for the court to say and another for the society/community to accept.

One of the upper caste decoy argument against reservation is that it should be economic/income criteria based rather than caste based. However, the oeuvre of Sen's approach is to show how poor the income criteria is for justice or even for something like 'development'.

> by proposing a fundamental shift in the focus of attention from the means of living to the actual opportunities a person has, the capability approach aims at a fairly radical change in the standard evaluative approaches widely used in economics and social studies (Ibid, 253).

This directly goes against the advocates of reservation based on income criteria. Income is just a means which can result in a culmination outcome and not a comprehensive outcome. It is not enough that the constitution declares that there is equality of opportunity. What matters is whether it exists actually? The capability approach has an information focus but it does not provide a formula as to what information has to be sought. That depends on the purpose at hand. I think, the information which is relevant with respect to caste, is social dignity and substantive opportunity. Sen says that sometimes one's freedom is dependent on others. Right to education is dependent on availability of school in the neighbourhood which no one parent can do. But social dignity is entirely dependent on others. A wealthy parent can establish a school or home-schooling but no single individual can achieve social dignity alone as it is dependent on others. Freedom from caste is not dependent on an individual but on the society or group.

Sen defines capability as 'being and functionings'. Caste is constitutive of being and either a hindrance or enabler of functionings depending on one's caste. This is a welcome advance from Indian career sociologists who portray caste as an empirical data.

Critique

Sen advocates a comparative approach in contrast to a transcendental approach of Rawls because it is closer to the reality. However, in the real world 'justice is what the court says'. The hypothetical case of the three children and the flute can be solved in a court of law in some manner. Sen himself indicates this by his advocating 'partial order'. The rate of income tax is another example. Income tax is basically taking away fruits of one's labour. It may so happen that the person giving the income tax may not be getting much of state services and those who are not paying income tax may be getting state services. The state simply levies a particular rate of income tax postponing any final judgement of a 'just rate'. This reveals the relation between power and justice. It is power which will come into being if justice becomes a Gordian knot.

Applying capability approach to aspects like education, health, poverty or famine which are amenable to quantitative measurement is rather easy. But applying it to caste, which is not amenable to quantitative measurement, is not easy. There cannot be much divergence of opinion on 'social issues' like poverty, health, epidemics but social stratifications issues like caste, race and gender have to encounter cultural relativism.

Sen starts from economics or discusses in the backdrop of economics. For example, he criticises rational-choice theory by saying that rationality cannot be coterminous with only self-interest seeking. But he does not use the word 'cultural relativism'. The solution which he will prescribe for resolving cultural relativism is public reasoning and the impartial spectator. However, public reasoning is not omnipotent and he partially recognizes this.

> it is of course true that many crude beliefs originate in some kind of reason—possibly of rather primitive kind (for example, racist and sexist prejudices survive often enough on the basis of the perceived 'reason' that non-whites or women are biologically or intellectually inferior) (Ibid, 35).

> no one, of course, expects that there will be complete unanimity in what everyone in the world actually wants and there is little hope that, say, a dedicated racist or sexist will be invariably reformed by the force of public argument (Ibid, 385-386).

As it was mentioned in the first section, Sen does not mention caste at crucial junctures. However, one can easily extrapolate from 'racist or sexist' in the above quote to casteist. Law as a coercive institution comes into being when public reasoning is not sufficient. Sen puts a premium on 'public reason' while Ambedkar puts a premium on law. Sen's criticism of Rawls is that people actually do not behave 'under a veil of ignorance'. But people also do not discharge their 'imperfect obligations' as well.

A comparative approach of justice with focus on capability appears to be much better than a transcendental approach to analyse caste. However, is Sen's approach, that does not compare between race and caste, comparative? He could have extricated himself from his Indian moorings and been the impartial spectator. Sen quotes extensively Wollstonescraft's criticism of Burke defending American independence bypassing the slavery issue. But he does not quote Ambedkar who criticised Gandhi along similar lines about Indian independence. Sen could have done that and it would have been of great help to all those fighting against caste injustice. Sen is reluctant to walk the last mile to justice.

> the way a person is viewed in a society with racial disparity may be deeply influenced by his or her visible racial characteristics and that can act a barrier to functioning possibilities in many circumstances. Distinctions of caste similarly have influences of their own, despite being frequently correlated with class (1995, 121-122).

Should we settle for correlation if we have the option of causality! Caste, race and gender are the historic causes which have given rise to class and not the other way round. These are the social ailments for which class is the symptom. Therefore, we have the option of either treating the cause or treating simultaneously the cause as well as the symptom. Reservation based on caste treats simultaneously the cause as well as the symptom while reservation based on economic criteria will treat only the symptom. It will be like paracetamol which will reduce the temperature but the underlying cause of fever will remain.

A crucial characteristic of discrimination will be 'unilateral hostility'. Caste, race, gender evoke unilateral hostility. Sen proposes unilateral obligation ('imperfect obligation') in asymmetric power situation as the solution. He gives two examples—human beings vis-à-vis animals and mother vis-à-vis child. Human and animal belong to two different species and mother-child relation is very different from upper caste-lower caste relation. It will certainly be good if the upper castes, who have disproportionately more power than the lower castes, accept some sort of 'imperfect obligations' towards the wellbeing of the lower castes. But acceptance of such perspective leaves lower castes at the mercy of upper castes—a la Gandhian approach. How realistic is it? Buttressing this further is a sort of functionalism found in Sen's emphasizing positive aspects of social norms.

> in dealing with such situations, there are two grand ways of bringing about the attainment of mutual benefits through cooperation, namely agreed contracts that can be enforced, and social norms that may work voluntarily in that direction (2010, 203)

Here Sen is emphasizing social norms. But social norms can be oppressive because the powerful might have devised them. The solution for this is to create a power equilibrium. The asymmetry of power will not disappear by Rawlsian 'veil of ignorance'. But it will not also disappear by emphasizing that the upper castes have unilateral obligation. Moving in the direction of power equilibrium may bring Marx or Ambedkar.

NOTES

1. Presented at the ICPR-TISS National Conference on 'Caste in India—Presence and Erasure', Tata Institute of Social Sciences, Mumbai, 20-21 January, 2014.

REFERENCES

Sen, Amartya, *The Idea of Justice*. Penguin, 2009.

Sen, Amartya, *The Argumentative Indian*. New York: Farrar, Strauss and Giroux, 2005.

Sen, Amartya, Jean Dreze, *India: Economic Development and Social Opportunity*. New Delhi: Oxford, 1995.

4

Inter Caste Marriage: Pain or Gain

As soon as Tina Dabi cleared the Civil Services examination topping it, Dalits were jubilant. They felt as if Tina Dabi taught a lesson to the Upper Caste merit morons. Next, Tina Dabi announced her love as well as intention to marry the number two, a Muslim, in the merit list of the Civil services examination she topped. By all accounts she came to know about the person only during training and not before. It was sudden love. This time some Dalits felt as if now they are taught a lesson by some sort of betrayal. However, they could not articulate rationally their uneasiness. Mere feeling, without a reason substantiating it, does not create injustice under the prevailing liberal models of justice. Though post modernism comes to the rescue of 'emotion', reason/rationality is still the king. Mere 'feeling' is not enough. It has to be justified by some reason to count. Following is the reasoning out of this feeling.

The Caste System and Inter-caste Marriage (ICM)

Theoretically marriage between two different castes of approximately same rank is also an inter-caste marriage (ICM). Hinduism does not prohibit ICM. In fact, it encourages one type of ICM—the hypergamy. Theoretically, if we take varna as the unit of comparison, then there can be 6 types of inter-varna marriage (IVM)—*shudra*—3, *vaisya*—2 and *kshatriya*—1. If we take caste, then it can be endless, as there are thousands of castes. It can be within the *Brahman varna* itself as there are different castes within the *Brahman varna* itself. However,

IVM between a lower and higher *kshatriya* may not result in as much bloodshed as between a *kshatriya* and a *shudra*. Thus, it may appear that inter-varna is the issue rather than inter-caste. However, it is the marriage between Dalit (SC/ST), who are theoretically *panchama* (outside the varna system altogether) and any other upper caste, that usually brings severe reprisal from the upper castes. Honour killing, which sometimes could be one's own daughter, is often the result.

This happens because theoretically, the de facto aim of the caste system is to place the *Brahman* male at the highest pedestal. This is achieved by encouraging movement of women upward in the hierarchy and prohibiting their downward movement. Foreseeing the danger of downward movement, Manu has already prescribed the status of the product of a hypogamus marriage (*pratiloma*) as lower than the man, thus dissuading any downward movement of women. This precludes theoretically an ICM that is also 'arranged'.

Love-marriage vs 'arranged' marriage

The moment ICM can be arranged, it can result in caste harmony because groups are involved. But to expect them to be arranged is to assume that stranglehold of caste is already loosened. Therefore, theoretical possibility for ICM will rest on love. Love transcending caste is based on the supposed premise 'love is blind'. Society too can pin its hope on 'love is blind'.

But a sociologist cannot just accept this social proverb without scrutiny. These proverbs are created to hide the ugly realities of society. A feminist can ask why should love be blind? Mimicking Marx we can say that it's not love that can alter social existence (caste system) but it is the social existence that creates love. Why the *Parsi* community has to launch a '*Jio Parsi* 'campaign to increase their population when they are surrounded by a population that is world famous for 'growth'! If love was natural, how come the *Parsi* population is dwindling! Besides other factors like hyper westernisation, it is also because the *Parsi* won't fall in love marriage easily with others.

Robert Merton reminded us that there are more than one side to a phenomenon. Love marriage between individuals is good for those individuals but can be bad for the community. Theoretically and conservatively, 50 per cent of the community has to probably suffer or die from backlash for the other 50 per cent to do love marriage.

Family and marriage, once supposedly a divine institution, have not been spared by feminists and Marxists. Only 'love' has been spared as a criticism-free zone; for example, there is no moral opprobrium if someone loves a Hitler-like individual. The Kerala High Court observed:

> Becoming a major gives them the authority to exercise all their rights as a citizen and once they attain the age of marriage, they can choose their partner. The choice may not be to the liking of the parents. He/she may opt for a criminal or a convict, a person of different religion, caste, colour, language or even decide not to marry at all. The parental authority in such instances is of a limited nature.[1]

But the limit of the transcending power of love is not explored. Can love transcend simultaneously caste, class and a host of other social factors including 'looks'? A cultural relative notion of beauty does not erase the category 'beauty'. 'White' or 'fair' plays a role in looks, probably because of historical domination of the west over the globe. Colour is almost a candidate as a stratification agent. 'Looks', which can be colour plus X (X stands for other culturally shaped criteria), is even more a candidate. Once we see through the limitation of love (is blind), the potential for love marriage to annihilate caste becomes much smaller.

Theoretically, in an arranged marriage, while the spouse's relations can be cool, the rest of the *maha-parivar* (extended family of the boy and girl) is supposed to be at good terms. Reality is very different. The 'arranged' in arrange means the dowry, not the good relation. Large-scale domestic violence and dowry violence in arranged marriages in the same *varna* point out the limitation of the arranged marriages even for inter-family harmony, what to speak of inter-caste harmony. Probably love between individuals has not created love between groups but rather much bloodshed.

It's not necessary that there will be a coming together in an ICM. There may also be a 'going away' as well. Besides, what if one side changes the side? Assuming the improbability and inability of changing side is underestimating agency. After all, the individuals first went for ICM exercising their agency. Why then, their progeny, would not exercise their choice by choosing the caste of mother or father? nothing is impossible. Wives routinely change to the side of the husband.

Anthropology has proved and now it is common knowledge that there is no pure race. There was always inter-racial marriage. But race as a social category has survived. The historian K.N. Panikkar makes a comment that there is no genuine *kshatriya* after 3rd century BC. Many *shudra*s became *raja* and then changed side and declared themselves *kshatriya*. It is for the individual consideration (love) that a *shudra* marries a *Brahman*. It is then profitable for the progeny to claim a full or half *Brahman* status and get all the privileges that go with it.

The Legal and the Social

That individuals are free to do inter-caste marriage is approved actually by law, not by socio-morality. The legal sanction for individuals doing inter-caste marriage is projected as a 'right' from a socio-moral point of view. However, what can be right from an individual-right point of view may not be right from a group-right point of view. This can be best illustrated by the tension between first and the third-generation rights. Amartya Sen in his book *The Idea of Justice* (2010) questions Arjuna's killing of the large number of his relatives. The maxim—'let justice be done even if the world perishes' may not be socially correct because what use would be the justice to the individual when the world has perished.

Liberal-Individualism and socialism

It is agreed that marriage (endogamy) is the crucial sustainer of the caste system. However, at the same time it is agreed that matters of marriage cannot be interfered with as that comes in the private personal sphere. Is a *Dalit* free to marry an upper caste? Obviously yes. But this is under a liberal-individualism (LI) framework. We must not forget that now liberalism accepts third generation rights (group rights). However, in a tussle, the individual rights are primary and supersede any community obligation. The goal is individualism—an autonomous individual.

Socialism has the goal of creating a better society. While the better society comes via the better individual in liberal-individualism (LI), the better individual comes via the better society in socialism. In socialism individual rights are not abrogated but they are subordinated and sometimes curtailed to social ends. Individual Dalits might have good relation with the upper castes e.g. *dharam-bhai* relation between upper and lower caste men. But Dalit and upper caste collective social interests are antithetical. It may not be the political and economic, but purely the status imbroglio. That is why such individual relations do not save them from atrocity just like individual good relations do not save the Muslim from communal depredation. Translated into the individual sphere the question becomes—can you marry your enemy? The answer is yes. The ground on which this can be justified is individual right. But if the question is should one marry one's enemy then the answer cannot be an emphatic yes. Historically many princesses married the marauders for saving the kingdom from depredation. It is only under a distorted liberal morality that one can justify—'let me marry, even if the world perishes'.

Conclusion

Under a liberal framework love marriage between individuals can become a cream skimming affair with the better off-in terms of looks, money and power-aligning with the better off leaving the rest to their fate or worse—to face the reprisal.

NOTE

1. http://www.livelaw.in/major-girl-may-opt-criminal-convict-person-different-religioncaste-marry-court-cant-resist-choice-kerala-hc/

REFERENCE

Sen, Amartya, *The Idea of Justice*. Penguin, 2010.

5

Escape from Caste Through Conversion: Is there a Way Out or a Way in?[1]

Various routes have been proposed to escape from the caste. The principal routes are the religious, the social and the legal. The case of the problem of caste is one of 'one leading to another'. Though untouchability is abolished on paper, it will go only with the abolition of caste. Ambedkar, in the *Annihilation of Caste* points out that abolition of caste requires destruction of endogamy which in turn requires the destruction of the authority of the Shastras. This means abolition of Hindu religion. Since that is not possible under a liberal framework, conversion seems to be the answer. However, that too has not worked much. Reflecting on this, this paper opines that there are two ways—a definitional surgery of Hinduism, and a comprehensive law taking care of indirect discrimination.

A significant proportion would not like to escape from caste

It is the lower castes who want to escape from caste just like it is the proletariat who would like to escape the class system. If we further extend the analogy of class then we can expect a polarisation of the OBC into upper and lower OBC. The 'upper OBC' may very well be satisfied with the caste system declaring themselves *kshatriya* which is the usual practice of underscoring social mobility in the caste system. On the other hand, the lower OBC, getting nothing from the caste system, would like the caste system to go. Thus, at the outset, a significant proportion of the population in the caste system would not like to escape from the system.

Really speaking, it helps if the upper castes convert rather than the lower castes. However, if we assume a gap between people's religious belief and their action, then we cannot assume that followers of a religion, that prescribes egalitarianism, will be actually practising egalitarianism in their day to day lives. This explains casteism among the Muslims and Christians in India. This is due to coexistence in a caste environment for centuries. If upper caste converts do not leave their discrimination to lower caste converts and non-converts, then conversion does not help the lower castes much. This is not to belittle the enlightening potential of conversion to lower castes themselves. But this does not reduce the violence by upper castes which is the reason to leave Hinduism in the first place. The violence has to be dealt with by law.

The difficulty of a long jump—Hinduism is not 'a' religion but a conglomeration of religions

Hinduism is not like caste. It is more like *varna*. Just like a *varna* is a conglomeration of castes, similarly Hinduism is a conglomeration of religions. The reason why Hinduism has been transformed into a conglomeration of religions is that what was supposed to be originally the name of a place has been transformed into the name of a religion (Sen 2006). Originally, Hindu meant what in contemporary parlance can be called Indian. Meghasthenes' *Indica* and Al-Beruni's *Al Hind* was the name of a place and not religion. Hindu meant those who lived in *Al Hind* just like *Mumbaikar* includes all those belonging to different religions living in Mumbai. 'The ancient Persians and Greeks called these people(s) "Hindus" and "Indikoi" respectively, and much later on, before and after the rise of Islam, the Arabs called the land beyond the great river al-Hind' (Lipner 2005, 4). 'The English word 'Hinduism" (and indeed "Hindu") is of comparatively recent coinage; there is evidence that it acquired some currency in the late eighteenth century in England' (Sweetman 2003, 56n12 cited in Lipner 2005, 5).

Since Hinduism originally didn't refer to any particular religion, therefore we do not find a god named Hindu. On the other hand, one can find a God called Brahma from which one can derive *Brahman*ism. Since Hinduism is not 'a' religion, there are ample contradictions within Hinduism ranging from asceticism to *Carvaka* philosophy. That's why reading Hinduism as 'a' religion in contrast to an assortment of religions will always run into difficulty. It's easy to criticise it as well as eulogise it focussing on particular parts. That's why the best definition that the judiciary can offer on Hinduism is 'a way of life'. Every religion will entail a certain way of life. But a way of life is not necessarily a religion. It begs the question—what kind of way of life? Can a caste-free Hindu way of life be imagined?

Defining Hinduism as a 'way of life' is not only an innocent inability, but also acts as an interpretive dominance. The interpretive dominance is used to define conversion of a tribal to Hinduism (from Christianity, Islam, etc.) as 'reconversion' based on the assumption that the original religion of the tribal was Hinduism (South Asia Human Rights Documentation Centre, 2008). In the legal sphere the juxtaposition of the historical (place) and contemporary meaning of Hinduism (religion) enables clubbing many religions of India under Hinduism. The approach can be called a residuary approach by which if someone does not belong to religions like Islam, Christianity etc. then by default that person belongs to Hinduism.

> Explanation II appended to Article 25 includes Sikhs, Jains and Buddhists as Hindus. The Hindu Succession Act of 1956, for instance, applies to:... (c) to any other person who is not a Muslim, Christian, Parsi or Jew by religion, unless it is proved that any such person would not have been governed by the Hindu law or by any other custom or usage as part of that law in respect of any of the matters dealt with herein if this Act had not been passed. (Sen 2006, 26; footnote)

Such interpretation is based on the premise that they share a lot. But just like racial intermingling happens through sheer co-existence for ages, similarly intermingling of religions has to happen through sheer circumstances of co-existence for ages. This does not mean that there are no separate religions. It can only mean that there is no 'pure religion' uncorrupted by others just like there is no pure race. Court judgements are prime example where quotations from more than one religion are used to buttress a single point or theme. Just because there are linkages between Hinduism, Sikhism and Buddhism doesn't mean that they are one and the same just like the way linkage between Judaism, Islam and Christianity doesn't mean they are considered as one and the same religion. In fact, Bronkhorst (2017) opines that Buddhism and Jainism cannot be traced to *Brahmanism* because of their different places of origin and different concerns.

> Buddhism and Jainism arose in a region far from the centre of Vedic religion, and their main concerns were altogether different from those that underlay Vedic religion. Buddhism and Jainism arose in the eastern parts of the Ganges valley... rebirth and karmic retribution, ... was clearly the central concern of these teachers and their followers, a concern that had nothing to do with the concerns that find expression in Vedic religion (ibid, 362).

Historically different religions were brought under Hinduism through a process which Mckim Mariott called 'universalisation' and 'parochialisation'. The case of Jagannath is an example. A forward linkage is established between Vishnu and Jagannath by declaring Jagannath as an avatar of Vishnu. At the same time through a backward linkage the origin of Jagannath is traced to Jagannath being worshiped by the *Saora* tribals. This is how practically the tribals are brought under the Hindu fold interpretatively. Similarly, a linkage is established between Hinduism and Buddhism by declaring Buddha as an avatar of Vishnu. Such interpretive coup is exclusion through inclusion.

One must indeed perform a very long jump to escape such

an all-inclusive definition of Hinduism. That's why opting for Buddhism, Sikhism, and Jainism won't create the desired socio-political effect because the converts purportedly will be still in Hinduism. Right wing adherents go a step further, play the double meaning of Hinduism (place and religion) and include even Christians and Muslims under Hindu.[2]

Conversion does not obviate the question of definitional surgery of Hinduism

Freedom of religion doesn't obviate the need to question the dominant definition of Hinduism. So far, theoretically, the strategy has been to accept the dominant definition of Hinduism and leave Hinduism to escape caste. But questioning the definition of Hinduism itself has not been a strategy.

If Hinduism involves both the 'great' and 'little traditions' (following Milton Singer) then conversion from Hinduism might involve leaving the 'little traditions' as well. The Lingayats have their own priest, the Jains their own Muni, the tribals have their own priest. A vast section of people has lived without the need for *Brahmans*.

It is better that people claim their own little traditions than leave them because of an overarching definition of Hinduism including them. Both the great traditions and little traditions are included in Hinduism. But if we separate *Brahmanism* (great traditions) from other local traditions then there is no need for leaving Hinduism. For example, the tribals at present have to leave their own religion technically and legally to leave Hinduism because *Sarna* is not legally recognised as religion different from Hinduism.

> The Hindu identity of tribes is an administrative creation of the Indian state ...Notwithstanding the long-standing demand for a distinct religion code for tribes, the state continues treating them as Hindus. (Xaxa 2017, 25).

If *Brahmanism*, *Sarna* and *Lingayat* are brought under Hinduism in the sense of 'Indic religions' then there is no need to leave Hinduism because in this case Hinduism becomes a classificatory word like 'Indic religions' and not a specific religion.

Under a liberal framework abolition of religion is not allowed but surgery is possible

The Indian constitution abolished untouchability through Article 17. However, it did not abolish caste system though it is the cause of untouchability. It protects *Vedic* Hindu religion, of which caste system is an integral part through the right to freedom of religion. Though untouchability is the highest degree of stigma and exclusion that can be attached to a group of castes, there are various types and degrees of stigmas attached to various lower castes. In fact, except the top two *varna*s like *Brahman* and *Kshatriya*, rest all are stigmatised to various extents in the caste system. Even, there are categories of stigmatised *Brahman* because they serve very low castes. Thus, from a human rights/dignity point of view, prohibiting only the extreme stigma like untouchability cannot be considered enough and it behoves of the law to prohibit the various levels of stigma as well. To achieve this, the whole caste system in toto needs to be abolished. However, that will involve virtually a denial of freedom of religion because caste system derives its legitimacy from *Veda*s, the most sacred books of *Brahmanism*. A liberal constitution cannot deny right to religion. For example, the courts have not declared the various personal laws based on different religions as unconstitutional violating right to equality.

Abolishing Hinduism is like abolishing Christianity in Italy—a tall order. Hinduism is the background religion for the Indian constitution and legal system. Only cow is mentioned and no other animal (Article 48). Some Hindu temples are even entitled to get state fund (Article 290A).[3] The central government sanctioned 50 crores for the *nabakalebara* celebration of Jagannath.[4] These are direct violations of maintaining arms length distance by the state from religion.

However, an historical example exists of surgery of religion to make it compatible to a liberal space. Mustafa Kemal Ataturk did not abolish Islam in Turkey. But he performed enough surgeries to make it compatible with a secular public space.

> On 1 November 1922, the Sultanate was abolished, on 29 October 1923 the Turkish Republic was proclaimed, and starting on 3 March 1924 a number of crucial laws leading to a series of institutional changes were passed: education was left to the monopoly of the state, the Caliphate was abolished and the religious schools (the medrese) were outlawed (Fuat Keyman 2007, 222).

In India, Pandit Nehru, unlike Kemal, didn't translate his enormous charisma into changing the society. But suppose he wanted, then his charisma would have been put to test because many around him were strong believers in Hinduism and the caste system. However, it is not as if no example exists in India of definitional surgery. In the Ramakrishna Mission (RKM) judgement (1986), the Calcutta High Court declared Ramakrishnaism as different from Hinduism and a religion in its own right. The argument by the RKM lawyers was that Ramakrishna founded a "universal" religion which was "meant not for the members of any particular caste, creed or religion but for the entire mankind" (Smith 1993 cited in Sen 2006, 19). The Court declared, 'In order to be a follower of Sri Ramakrishna, non-Hindus are not required to embrace Hinduism and to undergo *Suddhi* or some other form of purification. He could continue to profess and practise his own religion and at the same time be a follower of Sri Ramakrishna's faith' (Sen 2006, 20). Actually, the *Sarna* religion and many belonging to the little traditions will be much more fitting cases than Ramakrishna Mission for claiming independence from Hinduism.

Escaping caste through conversion is more a sociological matter than theological

Conversion to satisfy the religious and spiritual need and

conversion to escape from caste, which is a socio-political need, are two different things. The former demands a theological engagement while the latter a sociological one. Theological analysis will be mostly a textual analysis but sociological or historical analysis will not take the text at its face value. Theology won't question whether Ram existed or not. That is the job of history. The implication of *agni pariksa* on women's rights is not the job of theology but sociology. Thus, theology won't have a problem of proving tribals as Hindu on the basis of some ancient or medieval texts. But sociology will consider it a problem of declaring the *Dalit*/tribal as Hindu on the basis of certain texts which they themselves have not heard of. While constructing an all-embracing view of Hinduism one is legitimising texts which much of the masses might never have heard of. How many might have heard of the many *smriti*s except *Manusmriti* given the fact that *Dalits* were traditionally prohibited from studying in general and specially scriptures! Even *Manusmriti* was given a boost during colonial period. 'Whatever its historical status, however, most scholars today agree that it (*Manusmriti)* took on unprecedented status as an "applied" legal document only under early British rule' (Dirks 2001, 34). When Sir William Jones, who was a judge of the Supreme Court of Bengal appointed by the Crown, threw his weight behind *Manusmriti* as the Institutes of Hindu Law (Rocher 2010), *Manusmriti* acquired a status disproportionate to its actual stature in India in terms of people's awareness and acceptance of it in contrast to customs. This can be considered as the starting point of marginalisation of low caste and tribal customs under an all-encompassing definition of Hinduism.

Just like law on paper and law in action is differentiated, similarly religion as per the text and religion in practice should be differentiated. Why should my experience of Hinduism have less weight than Hinduism defined in some abstruse scriptures existing somewhere in Himalaya! Irrespective of any positive statements in the *Shastra*s about lower castes, the low castes have always experienced Hinduism the caste way. Therefore, even if caste is defined away as an aberration of Hinduism based on some *shastras*, the low castes have not experienced it like that and this should have some weight in defining Hinduism.

Once we move from theology to sociology, agency is shifted from intellectual elites to people. People must have a voice in defining themselves. Therefore, even if *Durga puja* is celebrated by all including the high castes, *Dalits* and tribals, the *Dalits* and tribals cannot be stripped of their right to deny themselves as Hindu. *No matter how similar I am to you I must retain the right to be me.*

Liberalism cannot destroy caste but it can blunt its sharp edges through robust rule of law

Annihilation of caste borders on a '3G (third generation) positive right' project. In a negative right the duty bearers are other individuals and the state. But in a positive right (socio-economic right) the duty bearer has to be exclusively the state. Caste doesn't exist at the individual level but exists always at a corporate/group level and therefore whatever solution has to be proposed about caste, that has to be always at the level of corporate/group like group inter-caste marriage or group conversion. But in a liberal framework the individual becomes the focus but not the group and therefore annihilation of caste is not possible within a liberal framework. It will restrict the limits to which state or group can interfere on the individual autonomy. If we assume individual agency (love marriage), then we should not forget group agency (arranged marriage). Sociologically the power of individual cannot be greater than that of group.

Caste is a stratifier. Empirically no stratifier exists in a pure form. We won't be able to find caste, class, gender or religion in a pure form in an empirical situation. It'll all be intermixed. Therefore, if one escapes from one stratifier, one may land up in another stratifier. For example if a lower caste stays in Hinduism, he is oppressed along caste. But if he moves to Islam or Christian, he might face oppression along religious lines. The Scheduled Castes lose the protection of Reservation and SC/ST (Prevention of Atrocities) Act 1989 when they convert to Islam or Christianity. It's like the case of a female who changes to a male by some technology to escape from oppression towards the female gender. But next he is called for military conscription because he is a male. Abolishing a stratifier then becomes a case of 'one leading to another'. There is not a discrimination free Shangri la. To top it all, these stratifiers at the same time are also identities. A liberal framework allows identity like caste which is a prized possession of individuals. Identities are mostly third generation rights like religion, caste, ethnicities etc. which gives the right to the group to have some control over its members.

Since one cannot abolish all the actual and potential stratifier-cum-identities, which liberalism will never allow, the next alternative is to remove the sharp edges of stratifiers which hurt people. This is the way in. When Kerala government appoints a priest on the basis of reservation, it's a case of 'way in', not 'way out'. But liberalism does not put all its faith on only civic virtue to do this. Those who think that civic virtue alone will eat away caste consciousness should remember that the rich can be oblivious of money, the powerful can be oblivious of power and the privileged can be oblivious of privilege. Sociologically speaking one takes note of the deviation, not the norm. The apparent sign of an absence of caste consciousness can be deceiving. The lower castes will always be conscious of caste. Civic virtue is welcome; but in case civic virtue doesn't work, there has to be rule of law.

This is what a comprehensive anti-discrimination law, which takes care of direct as well as indirect discrimination, does. The smartest way of discrimination and exclusion in a liberal society is the indirect way and not the direct way. Exclusion is mixed up with individual autonomy to make it difficult to separate and prohibit (Doyle 2007). This will be illustrated by the case of marriage. The caste system sustains through endogamy. However, the state cannot prescribe who to marry and who not to marry though a girl's acceptance or rejection of potential marriage partner may be based on caste consideration. Often it is brazenly mentioned in the marriage advertisements that SC/ST are simply not welcome as potential marriage partners. Under a liberal framework you are allowed to glorify yourself, but not at the expense of others. In a matrimonial advertisement you can write '*Brahmans* only', but you cannot write 'everybody else except the SC/ST' because that is denigrating to the SC/ST. This is what is casteism—glorifying own caste by denigrating others. Any 'ism' is simultaneously 'for' and 'against' something. The net result of all this is that the caste system and consequent stigma of lower castes continues through endogamy. This is how individual autonomy sustains social exclusion. Thus, a bourgeois-liberal law, standing guard for individual autonomy, may be the significant hurdle for social inclusion. Exclusion is perpetrated in the name of individual choice and autonomy. Marginalised groups are excluded from civic intercourse. They are prevented in an indirect way from housing ownership, rental market, club, jobs in the private sector etc. The dilemma is, to what extent individual autonomy is to be curtailed to promote social inclusion! While there is a vibrant legal discourse and laws redressing indirect discrimination in the west dating from 1971,[5] there is yet to be frequent academic discussion about it in India! It is impossible that Indian elite will be unaware about the legal developments in the west. But the lack of discussion of such remedy shows the elite apathy to provide suitable legal remedy for the marginalised.

Conclusion

Probably, over a long period, such a regime of anti-discrimination law will turn the caste to a 'difference' from 'identity' Something can be obnoxious as an 'identity' but not as a 'difference'. Privileges flow from identity but in 'difference' 'difference' ipso facto is the Privilege. We talk about caste, class, gender privileges but not privilege flowing from the latest fashion. When caste becomes a sort of 'difference', it becomes a sort of conspicuous consumption. When a *Brahman* NRI deals with an American in a discrimination free public sphere both identities work more like difference rather than identity as no privilege flows from it. The combination of civic virtue and rule of law will ensure that the constitutional morality of Ambedkar saps the caste ideal while more robust laws sap its material and behavioural basis.

NOTES

1. *Indian Journal of Dalit and Tribal Studies and Action* 2, Issue 3, No. 1 (2018): 1-9.
2. "Everyone born in India is a Hindu: RSS chief Mohan Bhagwat", *India Today*, https://www.indiatoday.in/india/story/everyone-born-in-india-is-a-hindu-says-rashtriya-swayamsevak-chief-mohan-bhagwat-959740-2017-02-08 Accessed on February 8, 2017.
3. Tahir Mahmood, "Articles of Faith", *The Indian Express*, September 13, 2017.
4. http://indianexpress.com/article/india/india-others/centre-sanctions-rs-50-crore-fund-for-nabakalebar-festival-in-odisha/ Accessed on March 21, 2015.
5. https://www.migpolgroup.com/old/public/docs/146.Limits andPotentialoftheConceptofIndirect Discrimination_EN_09.08.pdf

REFERENCES

Bronkhorst, Johannes, 'Brahmanism: Its Place in Ancient Indian Society'. *Contributions to Indian Sociology* 51, No. 3 (2017): 361–369.

Dirks, Nicholas B., *Castes of Mind: Colonialism and the Making of Modern India*. Delhi: Permanent Black, 2004.

Doyle, Oran, 'Direct Discrimination, Indirect Discrimination and Autonomy'. *Oxford Journal of Legal Studies* 27, No. 3 (2007): 537–553.

Fuat, Keyman E., 'Modernity, Secularism and Islam: The Case of Turkey'. *Theory, Culture, Society* 24 (2007): 215-234.

Lipner, Julius J., 'The Rise of "Hinduism"; or, How to Invent a World

Religion With Only Moderate Success'. *Lecture in the History and Philosophy of Hinduism.* https://www,jmu,edu/gandhicenter/wm_library/juliuslipnerlecture,pdf Accessed on October 13, 2005.

Rocher, Rosane, 'The Creation of Anglo-Hindu Law'. *Hinduism and Law: An Introduction* edited by Timothy Lubin, Donald R. Davis Jr., Jayanth K. Krishnan. New York: Cambridge University Press, 2010, pp. 78-88.

Sen, Ronojoy, 'Defining Religion: the Indian Supreme Court and Hinduism'. Heidelberg Papers in South Asian and Comparative Politics, 2006 http://archiv,ub,uniheidelberg,de/volltextserver/6936/1/Ronojoy_Sen_Defining_Religion_final_version,pdf Accessed on April 17, 2014.

Tobler, Christa, Limits and Potential of the Concept of Indirect Discrimination. European Commission, 2008. Http://Ec,Europa,Eu/Social/Blobservlet?Docid=1663&Langid=En Accessed on July 26, 2016.

6

Sociology of Education: Towards Inclusive Theorising[1]

Can we even talk of inclusive theorising?

What is inclusion? It can be defined as *remedial and preventive ways to counter discrimination and its effects.* Acts can be inclusive or non-inclusive. Is theorising an act? Yes. It is probably the most important and prestigious act in academics. There is the 'theory-fact' debate in social sciences. There is also a 'theory-act' debate, especially in education, where one is supposed to learn the theory in the university and act in the field (school). Theory is important for action while theorising itself is an important action. If theorising is an action then it can be inclusive or exclusive. The job of a theory is to make us understand by properly describing or/and explaining the situation. If it gives us a distorted view of a phenomenon by under or over-emphasizing particular aspects, then it can be charged with lacking inclusiveness, especially when the phenomenon in question is social. When a theory does not include the viewpoints of multiple social groups on a particular issue, it is discriminatory to those groups. It is a sort of perpetrator-less crime, which is the opposite of victim-less crime. For example, the theory of 'tribals as backward Hindu' by taking only the non-tribal view to the exclusion of the tribal view of themselves can be considered as an exclusionary act. This is exclusion by description. As a counter to such charges, often in academics, there is a 'subaltern view'. However, having separately a 'mainstream view' and a 'subaltern view' is not inclusive theorising because each doesn't include the other. In general sociology, there is something called a subaltern view. But the mainstream also masquerades as the subaltern view in sociology of education e.g. the concepts of cultural capital (Bourdieu), invisible pedagogy (Bernstein) etc.

Students in education read theories mainly from three disciplines—philosophy, psychology and sociology. Philosophy and psychology can talk about human beings in general but sociology of education is about discovering the context and the division in the society (stratification). So, psychology and philosophy are a little like natural sciences but the job of sociology of education is to describe and explain education in a contextual manner. That's why the issue of inclusion is a legitimate question in the context of theorising in sociology of education. One can talk about a transcendental philosophy but one cannot talk about a transcendental sociology. Psychological theories are supposed to be applicable anywhere in the world but sociological theories are supposed to be highly context specific. Therefore, when a particular sociology of education theory is propagated in a particular context like India, the question of it being inclusive or not is a legitimate one.

State of theorising in sociology of education

The theories of sociology of education start with the discussion of functionalism and then quickly move to Marxist inspired theories (Simons 2002) which is basically either school bashing or breast beating about how the education is aiding the domination of the dominant class. In this scheme of things, education as a medium through which the marginalised or the dominated class can do something about the domination is not inquired into.

In sociology of education, functionalism is considered conservative and Marxist inspired theories are considered radical or the view of the subaltern/marginalised. The major dispute between functionalism and Marxist inspired theories in sociology of education would be to see whether society is differentiated or undifferentiated. The functionalist would like to see the society as undifferentiated and the school serving all without harming anybody. The Marxist inspired theories would like to see the society as differentiated in terms of classes and see the school as an arm of the dominant class, which harms the working class. But Marxist inspired theories still do what Marx did albeit in a sophisticated way. They maintain that the school is still doing the job of aiding in domination albeit in a more sophisticated way. In a typical Marxist formulation, the school acts directly as an agent of indoctrination on behalf of the state which is considered as the executive committee of the bourgeoisie. In this formulation teachers cannot be given autonomy. The notion of 'Ideological State Apparatus' (Althusser 1972) improvises this and states that the school manufactures consent rather than directly indoctrinates.

> The 'Invisible Pedagogy' (Bernstein 1997) relies on weak classification and weak frames. Weak classification means that the invisible pedagogy does not emphasise on the clear-cut division like science, literature etc. It also means pupils are allowed to play, to do whatever they want, but only apparently. The teacher is in firm control of the context all the while. This is the strong frame behind the weak frame. Bernstein relates invisible pedagogy to the manipulation of frames as the new way of domination by the new middle class. The theory of invisible pedagogy brings out the subtle ways in which control is exercised in capitalist society (Khora 2011, 16).

Bourdieu[2] brings a host of innovative concepts to show that the education system serves the dominant class. This is done principally by generating a 'habitus' in education which matches with the habitus in other spheres like economy and the market. The school contributes to domination by masking or miscognising the actual objective class relations in the society. The relative autonomy of the school makes it worse as it portrays the school and education system as neutral, which further aids in the miscognising. Apple (1995) further refines the theory of cultural reproduction. For him technical/administrative knowledge is the cultural capital par excellence in the present age. Schools are not merely sites of reproduction but they are also the reservoirs of the cultural capital by appropriating it from their students and the society. Thus, the school is also a site of production of domination.

Henry Giroux (1983) is a little different. While Marxist inspired theories have a doomsday view of the school, Giroux tries to show how education can serve as an instrument of liberation instead of domination. He says that orthodox Marxist theory, the Functionalist theory, the theory of 'invisible pedagogy', 'hidden curriculum' and 'cultural reproduction'—have the following drawbacks:

- These theories, though pointing out the various insightful ways in which domination is perpetrated, do not paint a picture of hope. They portray 'domination through education' as a sort of fait accompli.
- They do not retrieve the subject from the dominance of structure. Since they do not define culture as 'lived experience' they also subject the subject to the dominance of culture.
- They do not take into account the factors of race and gender sufficiently. (Khora 2011, 19)

It may be noticed that Giroux has not mentioned caste. Obviously, because that is not his context. This is to show that a theory, no matter how good, is also circumscribed by the context in which it originates. If it tries to transcend too much the context in which it originates then it loses the descriptive and explanatory capacity to explain that context.

The Assumptions

It is not difficult to unearth the background assumptions of these theories. They can be mentioned as a mutually reinforcing package of notions/concepts as follows.

Liberalism/neo liberalism/capitalism/market/class

This combination is harmonious with Functionalism and an object of attack of Marxist inspired theories. The values and skills imparted by the school help one to survive in the market (Functionalism). The values in Functionalism are those conducive to order (value consensus) and not change. Parson's functionalism resting on value consensus looks like a social contract. However, this very aspect of the school—imparting values and skills—is construed as generating docility by Marxist inspired theories like Bourdieu's habitus. Bourdieu mentions that the habitus generated in the school also matches with the habitus in the market for symbolic goods.

Assumption of liberalism is manifest in the concepts emphasising domination in the indirect way rather than the direct way. This will be evident when we try to find the contrasting terms of these concepts as follows:

- Cultural capital—economic capital
- Invisible pedagogy—visible pedagogy
- Hidden curriculum—manifest curriculum
- Symbolic violence—physical violence

One can see that these thinkers have to take recourse to concepts that point out the indirect and sophisticated way of domination because liberalism does not allow such actions ab initio. Domination here means domination of one class over another albeit the concept of class is made more flexible to apply to an advanced capitalist society (Bourdieu).[3]

Instances of modification of theory incorporating context

Western theorists have kept pace and incorporated gender and race in their formulations. For example, Dillabough (1999) critiques the mainstream notion of teacher professionalism by applying feminism. The mainstream definition of teacher professionalism has masculinity built into it. It does not take into account the location of women who are saddled on the domestic front. Therefore, they can never be 'professional' if the dominant definition is applied. Therefore, the dominant notion must adjust and include 'emotion' too as a component of professionalism and not only 'reason'. Similarly Quiocho and Rios (2000) bring in a race and minority perspective to the sociology of teachers. While the mainstream perspective sees schoolteachers at the bottom of the status hierarchy, this is not so in case of minority/black teachers in their community. The minority teachers are looked up rather than looked down by minority students in contrast to middle and upper-class students looking down at schoolteachers. Kenway and Koh applied Bourdieu's notion of 'state nobility' to Singapore and found it wanting in some ways. To quote them:

> To conclude, the case of Singapore allows us to see what Bourdieu did not do. He did not conceive of fields that extend beyond the nation state or capitals with exchange value around the world. He did not see that elite schools could draw their prestige from the global hinterlands of a nation state as well as from the national field of power. He did not conceive of class or class relations that were not contained within a national field of power. And he certainly did not consider the possibility of a nobility unattached to a national field of power; in other words, a nobility without a state (2013, 287).

Coming to India—education/schooling in a caste society

Let's now see the consequences and the misfit of these theories when they apply to India, which is a very different context than the west. The broad perspective, which is applied in case of India, can be termed as the left liberal perspective—a sort of marriage between two incompatible partners. The tension will be evident when we apply it to particular issues that affect Indian education.

Quantity and quality of schooling

Functionalist and Marxist inspired theories assume a reasonable spread of schooling because their concern is to see what function the school performs or what the effect of schooling on society/stratification is. These theories will lose their potency if there is no widespread schooling, which was the case of India till the launch of *Sarva Shiksa Abhiyan* in 2000. Marxist inspired theories lament over the role of school in aiding domination. But the predominant concern in India so far has been to increase the quantity and quality of schooling. The position of Jyotiba Phule, Ambedkar or anybody from the marginalised section has been to increase the spread of schooling assuming that it is inherently something good for the marginalised. This is reflected empirically also where we see that *Dalit*-tribal have benefited from the spread of schooling.

A concomitant issue is regarding the advocacy of education through the mother tongue (Nambissan 1994). However, Kanungo and Mahapatra (2004) point out that the issue of mother tongue is not as simple as there could be 50 mother tongues in a single district. Leaving this apart, while education in the mother tongue is a constitutional right and the child best understands in the mother tongue, the left liberal perspective doesn't take a position regarding English. The state introduces English at a very early age considering the popular demand. While the elite reap the benefit of a very good English medium education, it preaches education in the mother tongue for the marginalised without taking into consideration the fact that English is the language of the power and the powerful. It is common in writings on education in India to lampoon Macaulay as the one who introduced a 'colonial' English medium education, supposed to be the source of much of our problem. The left liberal perspective derides Macaulay. Srinivasa Rao writes:

> 'However, the opinions of Charles Grant or Ram Mohan Roy did not have much effect till Thomas Babington Macaulay emerged on the Indian scene with his (in)famous Minute of 1835. As is well known, it is this Minute that set the systematic decline of both the classical languages of the day in India, namely, Sanskrit and Arabic, as well as numerous vernacular tongues. Firstly, it introduced English into the adrenalin of the Indian society, secondly it taught Indians as to how to be hegemonic over the other minority languages. (2008, 65).

Let's look at his footnotes as follows:

> 14- For contents of Macaulay's Minute of February 2, 1835, see Zastoupil and Moir (1999), p. 161–72.
>
> 15—However, it is not to suggest that the Indian elite were not hegemonic prior to Macaulay's era. Rather it was even worse, the manifestations of which can be found in the traditional caste system (ibid, 69).

In footnote 15 he acknowledges that the caste system could be even worse than British rule. However, he maintains his negative view of Macaulay, which is the dominant left view. This is not tenable if the minute of Macaulay, which is of 2-3 pages, is taken in totality. This is demonstrated by Bibek Debroy[4] and Chadrabhan Prasad[5]. *Dalit*s have benefited from the so called British system or Macaulay system of education. It is also to be mentioned that *Dalit*s have benefited from the Indian Penal Code, introduced by Macaulay, in place of *Manusmriti*. This may be the real reason why upper castes hate Macaulay. Similarly, drawing from Bourdieu, the lack of representation of the marginalised in the curriculum is portrayed as symbolic violence. This is true, but only to some extent. Education is not only about knowing the known but it is also an exploration into the unknown. The concept of symbolic violence cannot take into account the exploration into the unknown. The curriculum should not only include elements from the tribal culture, but also the Civil Rights Movement of the United States.

The Indian society is a caste society. Legitimacy is a concern in a class society because the backdrop is a liberal democracy. Therefore, there is a need for a concept like cultural capital to unravel the subtle domination. But caste is not bothered about any legitimacy at all because it does not grant formal equality ab initio. That's why education for the lower castes (*shudra*) is prohibited in a caste system. The school works as a legitimising instrument in class but overt hindrances are created for the lower castes to avail school in caste. The realities of *sanskritisation* are also the limits of the theory of cultural capital in a caste society. The lower class won't be openly assaulted for acquiring the cultural capital of the upper class in a class context, but in a caste context a lower caste will be brutally assaulted if they try to acquire the cultural capital of the higher caste (*sanskritisation*).

The left liberal perspective does a sort of camouflage act and doesn't answer the question 'whose side you are on'. The limit of this understanding is reached when Krishna Kumar (2011) explains away the coming into being of the Right to Education during the Neo-liberal phase of India by calling it 'ironical' without mentioning that a liberal regime is fully compatible with a rights regime. The left liberal view does not explain that the Right to Education, mentioned in the Directive Principles in the Indian Constitution, could not come for a long time because of the 'liberal limit' on the left policy of India. A Common School System was demanded which is basically a left perspective. But at the same time teacher autonomy was demanded which is basically a liberal perspective. Interestingly a common higher education system was not demanded which will involve questioning elite institutions like Jawaharlal Nehru University (JNU), Indian Institute of Technology (IIT), Indian Institute of Management (IIM), etc. which consume immense national resources and benefits immensely the upper castes. Theoretically, the left view can not give much autonomy to the teacher as the teacher has to act as an educator on behalf of the state. But the Indian left view share the liberal suspicion of state by advocating autonomy of the teacher from the state or autonomy of the curriculum from the state. This creates the undesirable position of wholesale teacher autonomy forgetting that autonomy can lead to discretion, which can lead to discrimination. This is reflected by empirical studies like Omprakash Valmiki's memoir of how he was harassed by the upper caste teachers or in contemporary times the sexual exploitation of girls in *Ashram Shalas*[6] by the teachers.

The notion of *Guru* (Hindu spiritual master) is another

issue on which the left liberal view in the sociology of education in India is ambivalent. For example, Krishna Kumar (2005) laments the transformation of the teacher into a 'meek dictator' during the colonial period but he is silent about what to do with the notion of *Guru*, which was and is prevalent. This notion is a glorification of the *Brahman* (Acharya 1996). Khora writes:

> The notion of guru contains historical as well as mythological baggage. The present day teacher is a British creation for the purpose of mass education. So, they can't be compared with the ancient gurus who always hobnobbed with the powers. The present day teacher is a successor of the teacher as a paid employee of the British period. The present day teacher operates under a framework decided by the state while the guru was not. The present day teacher lives fully in the society and society demands accountability from the teacher. It is not clear whether the guru was demanded accountability like the present day teacher. The guru was almost infallible. But the present [day] teacher is not considered infallible. She is rather considered as a facilitator of learning. While the guru-pupil relation was hierarchical, the present age emphasises democratic relation in the classroom. Education in ancient India was elitist, predominantly religious, teacher-centric all of which runs contrary to present values (2011, 179).

Krishna Kumar puts all the blame on the colonial period and thus sort of exonerates the period before the colonial. He does not engage with the issue that the *guru* must be tamed into a meek dictator if education to the untouchables is to be made available. Liberalism has to assume the rule of law. When there is rule of law, we don't expect overt discrimination and violence. While the Indian state may be based on liberal principles borrowing the constitution from liberal countries around the world, the Indian society is obviously not liberal. There is a difference between a liberal state and a liberal society. Different countries will be liberal to various degrees. The Indian society also can be called liberal but obviously it will be much less liberal then a European country or the United

States. The society-state mismatch will be much more in India than in case of western countries. If we assume this then we can visualise the limits of theories based on the assumption of a liberal society and state.

Conclusion

The important issues that we come across while discussing caste in education in India are—physical and sexual violence (in *Ashram shala*s), direct and indirect discrimination and violence at the level of school and higher education (Ramachandran, Naorem 2013). At the moment, some of the frequently occurring concepts in sociology of education are—'cultural capital', 'symbolic violence', 'hidden curriculum' and 'invisible/hidden pedagogy'. The distance of these concepts to the Indian realities is visible. If we include discrimination and violence as the starting point of theorising in the sociology of education in India, then the theoretical statement will look like the following.

- Instead of saying reproduction through education we can say reproduction by denying education through direct and indirect discrimination and violence.
- Instead of frequently saying class reproduction we can say caste reproduction.
- Instead of saying classroom we can say a bit rhetorically caste room[7].

NOTES

1. Presented at the National *Seminar on Ideas, Peoples and Inclusive Education in India Today*. Tata Institute of Social Science, Mumbai, 24 December, 2017.
2. Weininger, Elliot B., 'Pierre Bourdieu on social class and symbolic Violence'. https://www.ssc.wisc.edu/~wright/Found-c4rev.pdf Accessed on February 17, 2018.
3. Ibid.
4. Debroy, Bibek, "The Macaulay we don't know". *The Indian Express*, September 7, 2017.

5. Prasad, Chandra Bhan, "Mahatma Macaulay". *The Indian Express*, October 25, 2017.
6. The residential schools meant exclusively for tribal/indigenous children.
7. Term coined by S.R. Bodhi, Assistant Professor, Centre for Social Justice and Governance, School of Social Work, Tata Institute of Social Sciences.

REFERENCES

Acharya, Poromesh, 'Indigenous Education and Brahmanical Hegemony in Bengal'. *The Transmission of Knowledge in South Asia* edited by Nigel Crook. London: Oxford University Press, 1996, pp. 99–117.

Althusser, L., 'Ideology and Ideological State Apparatus'. *Education, Structure and Society* edited by B.R. Cosin. Harmondsworth: Penguin,1972, pp. 242–80.

Apple, Michael W., *Education and Power*. London: Routledge, 1995.

Bourdieu, P., 'The Forms of Capital', *Handbook of Theory and Research for the Sociology of Education* edited by J. Richardson. New York: Greenwood, 1986, pp. 241–258.

Dillabough, Jo-Anne, 'Gender Politics and Conceptions of the Modern Teacher: Women, Identity and Professionalism'. *British Journal of Sociology Education* 20, No. 3 (1999): 373–394.

Giroux, H., *Theory and Resistance in Education*. London: Bergin & Garvey, 1983.

Kanungo, Akshaya K., Hrushikesh Mahapatra, 'Tribal Education in Rayagada: A Review of Language, Textbook and Medium of Instruction'. *Orissa Review*, September (2004): 29–34.

Kenway, Jane, Aaron Koh, 'The Elite School as 'cognitive Machine' and 'Social Paradise': Developing Transnational Capitals for the National 'field of Power'. *Journal of Sociology* 49, No. 2-3 (2013): 272–290.

Khora, Sthabir, *Education and Teacher Professionalism*. Jaipur: Rawat, 2011.

—— 'Education Management in India the Need for Caution'. *International Journal of Research in Economics and Social Sciences (IJRESS)* 6, No. 8 (2016): 133-152.

Kumar, Krishna, 'Teaching and the Neo-Liberal State'. *Economic & Political Weekly* XLVI, No. 21 (2011): 37–40.

Kumar, Krishna, 'Meek Dictator: The Paradox of Teacher's Personality'. *Political Agenda of Education: A Study of Colonialist and Nationalist Ideas*, 2nd Edition. Delhi: Sage, 1991/2005, pp. 73–94.

Nambissan, Geetha B., 'Language and Schooling of Tribal Children: Issues Related to Medium of Instruction'. *Economic and Political Weekly* 29, No. 42 (1994): 2747–2757.

——- 'Equity in Education-Schooling of *Dalit* Children in India'. *Economic and Political Weekly* 31, No. 16–17 (1996): 1011–24.

Quiocho, Alice, Francisco Rios, 'The Power of Their Presence: Minority Group Teachers and Schooling'. *Review of Educational Research* 70, No. 4 (2000): 485–528.

Ramachandran, Vimala, Taramani Naorem, 'What It Means to Be a *Dalit* or Tribal Child in Our Schools A Synthesis of a Six-State Qualitative Study'. *Economic & Political Weekly,* XLVIII, No. 44 (2013): 43–52.

Simons, Maarten, 'Governmentality, Education and Quality Management Towards a Critique of the Permanent Quality Tribunal'. *Zeitschrift für Erziehungswissenschaft*, 5, No. 4 (2002): 617–633.

Rao, S. Srinivasa, 'India's Language Debates and Education of Linguistic Minorities'. *Economic & Political Weekly* 43, No. 36 (2008): 63–69.

PART II
RESERVATION

7

Patel Agitation and the Rationale Behind SC/ST Reservations[1]

The *Patel* agitation has reignited the anti-reservationists. The anti-reservationists thrive on popular, superfluous, ahistorical arguments about merit, justice and the state. The demand by well-off communities like *Patel*s, *Jat*s and others has created a sort of desert storm—that everyone deserves reservation. I will take up the following principal ahistorical arguments against SC/ST reservation and counter them. The main focus is on reservation in government employment here.

1. General category students feel discriminated when SC/ST with lower marks get the seats.
2. Merit is inherently good and should be the governing principle.
3. Economic criteria is better than caste criteria.

1. When do you feel discriminated?

People do not feel discriminated in a lottery when a single person gets a lot of money to the exclusion of all others because everybody has an equal chance to that jackpot. That's why recruitment without reservation is considered discriminatory because everybody does not have an equal chance.

A popular argument is that an upper caste student does not get a seat in spite of securing more marks than an SC/ST student. This may be valid, but only partially even if we assume that the backgrounds of both are the same. Let's assume a hypothetical situation where all the candidates have the same background. The upper caste student, who has not got the seat because an SC/ST with lower marks has got the seat, has three more avenues to blame. He could have secured more marks and got the seat like the other upper caste students, with same background. Statistically speaking, his chance is three times that of a SC as general quota is 50 per cent and SC is 15 per cent. If the reserved seats were potentially his, the general seats also were. Second, he also could have got the seat if the total number of seats was more. So s/he can blame the government for this. Lastly, he can also blame his *karma* and reconcile; after all, who can the SC/ST students, who do not get seats, blame!

When you succeed, you take the credit; when you fail, you can blame everything in this world. This happens practically too. It is possible that an upper caste fails in the civil service examination in the first attempt and blames reservation. In the second attempt, he gets a lower rank but now blames only himself. But in the third attempt he gets into IAS. Now no more need to blame anyone, only to take the credit for himself or for others like his parents. Somewhere else a coaching institute takes credit for the success. This also shows that merit, even though not present in the present, can appear in the future.

Apart from this, does an examination test merit for a job? If the examination was testing the merit for a job then why is there training before the job? This means that the examination was more of a 'fair allocation mechanism' than about merit for the job.

2A. Is merit inherently good?

Some say, there cannot be anything like good terrorism. Similarly, there cannot be anything like bad merit. However, popular discourse is full of merit gone wrong. The lawyer who can make false as true and true as false before the court, the computer hacker, the CA who can make black money as white and makes the least tax liability, the marketing man who can sell fridge to the Eskimo, the HR manager who can break the union—all these are cases of merit gone wrong or bad merit. In fact, the whole gamut of 'white collar crime' is basically merit gone wrong. Normally merit is defined as ability plus effort. But a third criteria is implicit—intention. The only problem is that there is no examination to figure out intention. It can be known only post facto. Only after that a corrupt official is removed.

Second, pure merit without fair allocative mechanism will lead to a heredity system rather than an egalitarian one. This must be happening to some extent but under respective categories of SC/ST, OBC and general quota. We can see what will happen if we remove reservation. Who else can be more meritorious for an IAS job than the son of an IAS who has some insights into the job from the inside? The father may also coach him. Wherever pure merit without a fair allocative mechanism prevails heredity rules; for example, film industry, politics, business. Therefore, merit worshipers are worshiping a false god.

2B. Group merit and representation ceiling

The merit discourse follows a Rambo approach to merit—a *deus ex machina* that saves the day. Barbara Kellerman's book, *Followership: How Followers Are Creating Change and Changing Leaders* (Harvard Business Press, 2008) tries to correct the one-sided view that, leader is everything and followers are nothing. What is required in a group is a team player rather than who believes in going alone. When we talk about bureaucracy, it is about group merit rather than individual merit.

In a limited pie scenario underrepresentation of some is integrally related to overrepresentation of some. This is the logic of land ceiling. A watch is kept over 'dominance abuse' in the market. It is the government which checks the dominance abuse in the market; but who will check the dominance abuse within the government? Some say that reservation has not brought the desired results. The explanation by the SC/ST is that they are not its principal implementers. If an upper caste secretary of social justice will be holding a grudge against reservation, how will s/he implement it wholeheartedly! Sufficient representation, which can be more than pro rata, is alright. But when sufficiency transforms to dominance it has to be checked.

The first merit of a group has to be representativeness. There is a saying, 'good government is no substitute for self-government'. How can people say 'our government' when only a few sections are dominant! The dominance of a few in a group distorts its actions. The Punjabi dominance in Pakistan, the Jew dominance in USA—all these distorted their actions. The first contributed partially to its own break-up. The second continues to be partially responsible for the misery of Palestine. In India, underrepresentation of certain communities in the police make it behave in a certain way.

3A. Is economic criteria better?

Some argue that since everybody is asking for reservation in the name of caste let's have reservation on economic basis. But poverty in India is not a variable but constant. Except a few, everybody is poor. Therefore, even under economic criteria everybody will demand reservation.

But the ulterior motive of proposing economic criteria could be its susceptibility to fraud and manipulation. Even caste certificate is frauded. But it has an inbuilt disincentive. An upper caste has to pay the social ignominy to pass off as a SC/ST. When we propose certain criteria, we have to see the probability to fraud. India's high rank in Global Corruption Index shows the probability of corruption. *Vyapam* shows the sophistication. Economic criterion will be easily frauded. This is evident by the fact that only 4 per cent pay income tax in India compared to 30-40 per cent in developed countries. The Income Tax department periodically issues warnings. The size of black economy which is considered equal to the formal economy is a proof of this. Periodic amnesty schemes for black money are an admission of the difficulty to control the economic criteria. Income changes from moment to moment. Even if someone has 50 acres of land, he can keep it fallow for one year, show the minimal income for that year, and thus will be eligible for reservation. How can reservation, which is relatively stable, be based on something fluctuating like economic criteria!

Theoretically caste is considered 'particularistic' and economic criteria like income are considered 'universalistic' because it can cut across gender, caste, religion etc. It is considered ethically superior because of this feature. However, it is this very feature that can become its nemesis. Any measurement method is meaningless if it is prone to error beyond certain level. While the error on caste criteria can be of undeserving groups muscling in, that on economic criteria will be of undeserving individuals. The error in income criteria will always be more than caste because individuals are always more than groups. The error on economic criteria can be theoretically 100 per cent, as even a millionaire can give away all his money and become a pauper deserving reservation.

The litmus test for the economic criteria will be a hypothetical comparison between a *Brahman* and a SC/ST daily wage labourer. Assuming there is one job (assuming scarcity), who should the job go to? Assuming that the external social world is discrimination free, the difference remains of their inner 'contentment'. The *Brahman* at least has the self-satisfaction of being born into the highest caste while the SC/ST will be cursing himself of being born into the lowest caste. He is doubly cursed—economically, socially.

How can exclusive economic criteria take care of caste discrimination? When a father can kill his own daughter in the name of caste honour, how can we assume that there can't be any caste discrimination even if the income remains the same for upper and lower caste candidates. There is a chance that the upper caste selector may favour an upper caste compared to a lower caste having same economic background in an interview. The macro effect of exclusive economic criterion would be that upper castes, albeit poor, will capture the present reserved seats in a manipulated game of merit.

Exclusive economic criteria portray as if government jobs are only about livelihood, not power. A government job has three aspects—livelihood to the holder, service to the people and governing people which involves power. An IAS job is not merely one individual's livelihood. It is a job affecting others' livelihood. A police inspector's job is not only about his/her livelihood but about justice for others as well. Those who portray economics as everything forget that Muslims and SC/ST may not get houses in certain areas even if they have the money.

SC/ST reservation is not only about material compensation or representation but also an apology from upper castes that assuages the humiliation of SC/ST for the historic oppression. When reservation is abrogated, not only the extremely modest reparation vanishes but also it makes it seem as if nothing happened in the last 2,000 years. This aspect is not substitutable by caste neutral economic criteria.

Even if reservation is completely abolished there would still be poor *Brahmans* unemployed. What about them! Liberal frameworks do not guarantee 'right to work'. That is done by socialist framework. Those who are shouting for economic criteria, are they ready for this?

3B. Industry, trade, big agriculture—the real *damads* (sons-in-law)

SC/ST are lampooned as *damads* of government. But there are other *damads* of government. The first and foremost is the industrialist who gets land, power, mineral resource, finance at cheap rates. Import of capital equipment is duty free. There might be a tax holiday on the income. After many years the loan may become NPA because the meritorious Chartered Accountant might have proved that the company was making loss for past 10 years. The second *damad* is the big agriculturist having hundreds of acres of land, may be half of it *benami*.

The landed agriculturist gets water, electricity for free or at very cheap rate. He also gets fertiliser subsidy. The MSP is there to take care of the produce defying the market. To top it all, even if the income can be substantial, there is no income tax on agricultural income. There is a chance of loan waiver after some time. This could be the reason why the *Patel*s have become so strong. SC/ST have very little presence in industry, trade, big agriculture and many other spheres like cooperatives. Reservation will be eclipsed compared to what concession/subsidy government gives to these *damads*. But the SC/ST are lampooned to have the habit of eating free.

It is some of these powerful groups, who having benefited immensely from the post-independence subsidy economy, are now saying: reservation is our right, we are going to snatch it. When *Dalit adivasis* say that *jal, jangal, zamin* is our right, and we are going to take it, then they are told to adopt constitutional democratic means. Some have to abide by the constitution and some are above the constitution.

3C. Caste ++ criteria

A variant of the economic argument is what can be called caste++ argument—caste along with economic and other criteria to better target the most marginalised among the *Dalit*. The repercussion will be prevention of elite formation within the SC/ST. But the larger repercussion of such exclusive measure only with respect to SC/ST category to the exclusion of general category will be—(1) power imbalance in the society, (2) injustice to non-elite upper caste. The elite-targeting assumes that the role of elite can only be bad, not good. Ambedkar became an elite (in terms of knowledge, not money or power) through the help of another elite the Gaikwad of Baroda. But certainly, he did immeasurable good to the lower castes. Usually it is the elite upper castes who oppress the non-elite SC/ST and it is the elite SC/ST who come to the aid. Without the SC/ST elite, reservation will be in danger as reservation sustains not only through arguments but through balance of power.

Conclusion

SC/ST category is the pivot of the constitution in India. Reservations alone do not define the SC/ST category. There is a whole constitutional and government architecture built on the category of SC/ST—political reservation, untouchability (Art 17), 5th schedule, 6th schedule, commission for SC and ST, education and employment reservation, Special Component Plan, Atrocities Act etc. The judiciary has to decide whether these are part of basic structure or not before proceeding to change it. All these are linked together by one rationale that there are some sections of society requiring special measure for some very concrete reasons. When protection to the weak is abolished then the *eminent domain* becomes the eminent demon. The social contract becomes null and void. Abolition of the category will create a chain reaction, the end result of which will simply be catastrophic. After the big architecture of reservation is gone, it will be a minor matter to finish off Article 29 for minorities, the personal laws, any special provision for Jammu and Kashmir etc. Two countries will be happy about the chaos—Pakistan, China.

NOTE

1. *Round Table India,* 21 October, 2015. http://roundtableindia.co.in/index.php?option=com_content&view=article&id=8377:merit-fetish-intelligence-flight-and-deserts-storm&catid=119:feature&Itemid=132.

8

Reservation and the Creamy Layer Principle: Solving the Puzzle[1]

The issue of creamy layer among SC/ST has finally reached the Supreme Court.[2] There is no escape from debating this issue now. Social issues always have more than one side. The issue of creamy layer has already been discussed by a few—against creamy layer (Chaudhury 2004; Srinivas 2007; Sundaram 2007) and justifying it (Pandian 2000; Subramanian 2006). This article will discuss hitherto undiscussed ramifications of applying creamy layer to SC/ST reservation in government employment.

A government job is a combination of three aspects—livelihood to the holder, service to the people and power conferred for doing the service

The creamy layer principle sees government jobs predominantly as a 'benefit'. But a government job has three aspects—livelihood to the holder, service to the people and power conferred for doing the service. The higher the job, the higher the service and power quotient but lower the livelihood quotient. Livelihood aspect of a collector's job is much less salient in contrast to a class IV employee. Reservation is considered as 'benefit' only focussing on the livelihood aspect. People have a tendency to slip into naming reservation as a benefit. Yogendra Yadav writes:

> This would mean, for example, that the privileged among the SC are not excluded altogether from the benefits of reservation but

> are placed at the end of the queue. They get to enjoy the *benefits* of reservation only if there are slots left after the non-privileged SC candidates have been accommodated.[3]

Of course, elsewhere he does not forget to mention the power dimension. This is just to show that we slip into naming reservation as a benefit. The justification of each component is based on different justifications as follows.

Power—The sole justification for suitability is *representation*. For example, one does not raise the issue of merit in the usual sense of educational qualification etc. in political representation, which is about power sharing. Identity is prime qualification here. In group representation none should be under-represented. But a corollary to this is that none should be over-represented as well. The reasons why none should be under-represented is two-intrinsic (as a democratic value), instrumental (to take care of their interest). For these two reasons there should not be over-representation of any group as the over-represented group is likely to take care of its interest disproportionately.

Livelihood—Here the suitability is the degree of economic deprivation.

Service/job—Here the suitability is so called merit. One should bear in mind that the name is 'civil service', not individual gratification. However, 'civil service' in India is more of a 'fair allocation' than merit in the sense of 'likelihood of performance'. There is no logical link between one's performance in 'Pali' or 'Sanskrit' language and the job of a collector.

Opportunity always means opportunity to live, not die. We don't agree with statement like 'I am giving an opportunity to you to die'. This means that people are competing for the livelihood and power quotient of the jobs than the service quotient. That's why there is shortage of people for jobs in armed forces though it provides a good economic package. It is the state's interest that you serve well. 'Opportunity to serve the country' is a suitable answer in the interview. This cannot be raised to the level of truth because there is another saying, 'power corrupts'. The creamy layer restriction is not applicable to power (representation) and service aspects of government jobs (bureaucracy). For example, with respect to power sharing aspect, we cannot complain about industrialists becoming MP, MLA and serving the country. Thus, when upper castes are talking about 'equal opportunity' they are only asking the benefit (livelihood) and power part of a job and not the service part.

Who is the most deserving—deprivation vs contribution

There are two ways we can decide who is the most deserving for the reservation—retrospective and prospective. In a backward move, we have to see who has suffered the most and in a forward move we have to see who is going to do justice to the job. If we look backward then the most deserving might be dead. Actually, the forefathers of SC/ST, the most deserving, because they suffered, are dead. In the present time many who get *Param Vir Chakra* get it posthumously. Creamy layer is applicable only to this aspect and not in the aspect of contribution. Deciding who is the most deserving has to be a balancing act between deprivation and contribution. The person most deserving from the deprivation point of view may not have requisite contribution capacity for the 'service'.

Creamy layer is justified to kick in when existing quota is filled to the brim and there is pressure outward

The issue of someone taking from someone else's seats arises when there is no vacancy. But one of the excuses given for widespread vacancy of reserved seats is non-availability of suitable candidates. In fact, earlier such seats were converted to general category. Even now in class I and II jobs SC/ST reserved category is not fully filled up.[4]

Secondly, if poor SC/ST complain about economics as the roadblock, then government has many schemes in the form of scholarships, hostels, coaching etc. to aid them in competing.

Nothing stops the government to better these schemes quantitatively and qualitatively.

Representation—quantitative and qualitative

So far reservation/representation is predominantly constructed in a quantitative manner. It has not been thought of in a qualitative manner. What matters is not only quantity of representation but quality of representation. If one were to figure out the creamy layer of the Indian state, then it would be higher judiciary, scientific and technical personnel and defence. This is the real creamy layer. There is no reservation here though ideally there should have been because these are the prime levers of power. 'General' would be dominant here because the creamy layer debate starts with the assumption that creamy layer captures. This can be inferred from the fact that the SC/ST have very little presence in the higher civil services.[5] Only 'creamy layer-Scheduled Caste /Scheduled Tribe' has some possibility of trickling in to this 'general-creamy layer'. If there is no reservation in the 'general-creamy layer' then preventing SC/ST ab initio in to this through creamy layer restriction is injustice.

If there is a notion called 'group merit' then there can also be a notion called 'group threshold'. If a SC/ST becomes IAS at the age of 33, his individual problem is over. But group problem is not over until a SC/ST reaches to the level of secretary of social justice department. That can happen only if s/he clears IAS at age 21. The probability of such a happenstance is greater only among creamy layer SC/ST.

Who is entitled to define which sphere has to be reservation free? 'We the people', which is supposed to have given us the constitution, will look vacuous if we strip it of Scheduled Castes/Scheduled Tribes. Thus, reservation is not a 'benefit' given by non-SC/ST to SC/ST but SC/ST themselves are entitled as part of 'we the people' to define the scope and contour of reservation.

Pitting 'Creamy layer SC/ST' against 'creamy layer general' violates principle of equality

Creamy layer is about bringing a class framework in the form of economic criteria. The constitution uses the word caste and tribe in case of SC/ST and class in case of OBC. Everybody is 'free' to compete in the 'general' category. Free automatically doesn't mean 'fair'. Therefore, we say 'free and fair' election. We use the word 'free market' and 'fair price'. The general category is not caste based. Thus, one can bring class framework in it. Therefore, it is constitutionally permissible to bring class in the sense of economic class into the OBC and general.

Additionally, 'creamy layer SC/ST' won't be competing against the 'general-general' but the 'general-creamy layer'. The creamy layer debate presumes that the creamy layer corners most of the jobs within a particular category. This must be true in case of general category as well. When a 'creamy layer SC/ST' will be thrown into the general category then they will be competing not against the 'general-general' but the 'creamy layer general'. This will be the point of injustice. Pitting 'creamy layer SC/ST' against 'creamy layer general' violates the principle of equality. It's anybody's guess whether they will stand a chance. This can be rhetorically represented as: 'in SC/ST there is a creamy layer, but the general category is full of cream'.

Continuous hierarchy or discrete categories

Sociology students are familiar with these terms of Professor Dipankar Gupta. The general, the OBC and the SC/ST can be seen as a hierarchical system of roughly the upper castes, the middle castes, and lower/untouchable castes. If you treat this as continuous hierarchy then you should apply any principle to the three categories and not just one category; for example creamy layer. *In this scheme there will be a creamy layer in each category.* On the other hand, if you treat the three as discrete categories then a person belonging to one category cannot belong to another category. *SC/ST belonging to creamy layer are still a sub-category of SC/ST*. They do not become general.

If the general category is treated as a residual category devoid of caste, class and gender, then any SC/ST qualifying under that category is no more SC/ST but general and for analytic purpose loses his/her caste status. You cannot then claim that some well-off SC/ST are taking away the general seats. In fact, while deciding the deserving in the general category one has to be caste, class and gender blind. An SC/ST can qualify only once—either in general category as general or in reserved as SC/ST. So, the creamy layer getting a double chance argument does not hold.

One can go in two ways—group way and the individual way. Mixing both can create problems. You cannot only bring class into the caste but any other stratifier like gender. Bringing too much of individual rights destroys a group right. When we create a group right, we have to refrain from applying too much of individual rights. Otherwise the group right can be taken away by applying individual rights. This is giving with one hand and taking away with the other.

Beyond economics—the social and cultural capital

Economic criteria like income are discredited in economics itself where the current fashion seems to be 'inclusive growth', 'inclusive development', 'human development index' etc. Legally speaking a person may earn crores, but you cannot impute that to his married daughter though practically he may support his daughter all the way.

The legal problem arises only when law takes cognizance of only the economic capital. An SC/ST and general of same income is equal only if everything else is same. But, if judiciary takes cognizance of social and cultural capital, which is well accepted in social sciences, then it probably will hesitate to equal a *Brahman* and a Dalit with equal income because cultural and social capital of both will differ widely. Empirically this can be brought out by posing a question: after becoming IAS, which group the SC/ST belongs—the SC/ST group where there is a sprinkling of IAS or the 'general' group of IAS! They will be nowhere close to the social capital (network) of a *Brahman* IAS given that the creamy layer of the Indian state is a 'general-creamy layer'.

NOTES

1. *Round Table India*, 14 July, 2018. https://roundtableindia.co.in/index.php?option=com_content&view=article&id=9415:reservation-and-the-creamy-layer-principle-solving-the-puzzle&catid=119:feature&Itemid=132.
2. Rajagopal, Krishnadas, "In a first, plea in apex court seeks SC/ST creamy layer's exclusion from quota", *The Hindu*, January 28, 2018.
3. Yadav, Yogendra, Rethinking social justice, http://www.india-seminar.com/2009/601/601_yogendra_yadav.htm Accessed on July 2, 2018.
4. "SC/STs fail to break caste ceiling: No SC in 149 top government officers, 40 pc do menial jobs", https://economictimes.indiatimes.com/news/politics-and-nation/SC/STs-fail-to-break-caste-ceiling-no-sc-in-149-top-government-officers-40-pc-do-menial-jobs/articleshow/16278743.cms Accessed on July, 2018.
5. http://pib.nic.in/newsite/PrintRelease.aspx?relid=132395 Accessed on July 2, 2018.

REFERENCES

Chaudhury, Pradipta, 'The Creamy Layer'. *Economic and Political Weekly* 39, No. 20 (2004): 1989-1991.

Pandian, M.S.S., 'Reservation Policy: Myth of Creamy Layer'. *Economic & Political Weekly* 35, No. 17 (2000): 1417-1417.

Srinivas, K. Ravi, 'Demystifying the anti-Creamy Layer'. *Economic & Political Weekly* 42, No. 04 (2007): 327-328.

Subramanian, S., 'Examining the 'Creamy Layer' Principle'. *Economic & Political Weekly* 41, No. 45 (2006): 4643-4645.

Sundaram, K., 'Creamy Layer Principle: A Comment'. *Economic & Political Weekly* 42, No. 4 (2007): 326-327.

9

Creamy Layer: Jurisprudence in the Air[1]

Rudolf von Jhering as a reaction to Puchta contrasted 'jurisprudence in the air,' with 'jurisprudence of realities'. Drawing from Savigny's connection between law and other aspects of social life he construed that law had been produced by efforts to realize a social purpose. Such a purpose was always practical. Law had then to be understood as a means of realizing an objective that was both social and practical. The creamy layer judgement *Jarnail Singh vs Lachhmi Narain Gupta* on 26 September, 2018 appears like a jurisprudence in the air.

There are two reasons why people are scared of analysing Court judgements. One is purely physical—the contempt of court and jail. The other, intellectual fear, is that a court judgement must have been arrived at after deliberation by great minds and therefore it may not be possible for ordinary mortals to analyse and find some flaw in it. This is unfounded because while the judges might have a vast background in case law it is not easy for them to have enough knowledge in sociology because of lack of time. Breaking of fresh ground happens not through case law but through philosophy or sociology. I will begin by quoting one passage from this judgement.

> Equality has two facets—formal equality and proportional equality. Proportional equality is equality in fact whereas formal equality is equality in law. Formal equality exists in the rule of law. In the case of proportional equality, the state is expected to take affirmative steps in favour of disadvantaged sections of the society within the framework of liberal democracy. *Egalitarian equality is proportional equality* (para 103; emphasis added).

The last sentence is difficult to make sense of. What do you mean by egalitarian equality! The court shows that it is much concerned with substantive equality. But if creamy layer is intrinsic corollary to the equality principle then how can general category be exempt from it? Is parliament competent to apply creamy layer principle to the general category? If the court is reading substantive equality in Article 14, why it is not accepting indirect discrimination which happens in the promotion of SC/ST employees! When someone arrives at the collector's post through reservation in direct recruitment through the IAS, doesn't violate equality principle. But when one arrives at the same post through reservation in promotions through the state civil services that violates the equality principle! What sort of logic is this!

Creamy layer—when do you call something a 'layer'?

At what level something is justified to be called as a layer? If there are five well-off individuals out of 1,000, then are we justified to say it's a layer! Taking biological analogy you do not call a person with some fat just on the tummy as 'fat'. You call 'fat' a person only when he is above 15 per cent fat which is all over the body. But if you prescribe serious dieting to a person with just 5 per cent fat, you really endanger that person because some amount of fat is the sign of health of that person. The supreme court is not happy with one per cent fat of SC/ST and is prescribing a rigorous diet that is actually suitable for the general category.

SC/ST are class in a sociological sense and not statistical sense

The Supreme Court's logic is that income and status of SC/ST IAS, IPS is so different from the rest of the SC/ST that they no more belong to that class. By this logic the Supreme Court Judges cannot be Indian because the privileged life they live is not lived by 99.99 per cent Indians. SC/ST are class in the sense of community and not in terms of statistics (income).

The prime criterion of something to be called community is 'we feeling' (as per sociology). In that sense the Supreme Court Judges are also Indians and SC/ST IAS are also SC/ST.

The court has given example of IAS and IPS. Suppose SC/ST IAS and IPS give testimony that they still face discrimination and they don't feel that their status has been rising, then will the court accept that? The court simply makes statements like 'when an SC ST will become IAS/IPS the person has no problem (social backwardness gone)'; but it doesn't quote any study nor does it even recommend the Social Justice Department to conduct a study.

The criteria of inclusion and exclusion must be the same

The class of SC, ST, OBC was not constituted on economic basis. Therefore, post facto you cannot apply economic criteria to decide whether an individual belongs to that class or not. The criteria to include and the criteria to exclude must remain the same otherwise there is discrimination. Not applying creamy layer at the entry stage but applying at the promotion stage is this type of discrimination.

How will the Supreme Court handle it? By including it in the entry stage as well about which already there is a petition.[2] The present judgement sort of prepares the ground for it. This is two wrongs equals one right. Ambedkar, frustrated with Gandhian logic—upper caste atonement only rather than depressed caste resistance as solution for untouchability—said, 'this is not Aristotelian logic, but Mahatmian logic'.

Difference between OBC, SC and ST

The whole logic starts with the premise that the creamy layer notion related to OBC is equally applicable to SC/ST. While applying the same to SC/ST the Supreme Court should mind that they are two species apart. The differences are—5th schedule, 6th schedule, Article 164(1), PCR, Atrocities Act, SCP and may be many more.

When 52 per cent OBC are given just 27 per cent reservation, there can be a presumption of scrambling for jobs and creamy layer taking away non-creamy layer's jobs. but in case of SC/ST, the reservation is in proportion to their population and therefore why should it be assumed that the creamy layer should be taking away non-creamy layer's jobs? the actual situation is just that. SC/ST quota is never fully filled up.

Efficiency/Merit

There are three spheres where there is no reservation—defense, higher scientific and technical personnel and higher judiciary. I will focus on the efficiency of these.

Efficiency of the higher judiciary—Courts should be the last to talk about efficiency. You can know efficiency either quantitatively or qualitatively. The quantitative aspect about pending cases is known to everybody. How to judge the qualitative aspect? one way to figure out the merit of higher judiciary is whether they have written any jurisprudence books (not merely a compilation of case laws), which is respected all over the world like Justice Holmes. Talcott Parsons while addressing before some law students told that it's difficult to find tolerable consistency in the case law. Therefore, compilation of case laws (commentaries) is not an acid test of judicial acumen. Our judges mostly write biographies.

If there is a presumption that those who score less in an open competition have less merit then what will be the presumption about those who do not even face any competition! In the collegium system there is neither openness nor competition. How can it then be presumed that they have more merit compared to others! If somebody has really confidence, that person won't shy away from competition.

Efficiency of higher civil service—The very premise of judicial activism is executive inefficiency. That apart, judiciary's comment on executive efficiency violates the separation of power principle. What level of efficiency or inefficiency to be tolerated is up to the government to decide. If the government is inefficient, which I think it is, the whole people will bear it.

No violation of equality principle. This is illustrated by the recent lateral recruitment at the joint secretary level. When the state does lateral recruitment at the level of joint secretary in the name of efficiency then it's purely an executive matter but when the same state provides for reservation at the level of joint secretary then it is not executive matter anymore!

What part of government has to be reservation free? By court's own logic it is 'the speciality and super speciality'. The whole higher civil service is manned by the IAS generalists and not some specialists.

Reservation can never be a benefit for the individual or group but only be about representation

The court has used 'representation' and 'benefit' in the same breath. If it is representation then the question of benefit is immaterial. That the same job of a collector held by an upper caste becomes public service but when held by a SC/ST becomes a benefit is itself a discriminatory attitude.

The rationale of reservation at the entry stage and in promotion at present can only be representation. This is the rationale flowing from Poona Pact (1932). Contrary to popular opinion it cannot be linked to individual or even community upliftment. The judgement mentions

> The whole object of reservation is to see that backward classes of citizens move forward so that they may march hand in hand with other citizens of India on an equal basis. This will not be possible if only the creamy layer within that class bag all the coveted jobs in the public sector and perpetuate themselves, leaving the rest of the class as backward as they always were.

Put it simply, the creamy layer forgets reservation which in turn is used by the next in line and that's how the whole community will do a forward march. Considering the few or none govermment jobs, does the court have any idea as to how many years it will take for the community to attain some improvement! Do a few government jobs lift an entire community? This is theoretically next to impossible. So, discussion about this path of improvement is meaningless. This is some sort of notion that if one saves enough one will be rich without focussing on what's the income.

There is another reason why reservation is not about the community's welfare. The welfare argument is theoretically true if the SC/ST are employed exclusively for the welfare of SC/ST. But this is not how the government works. The government works as a whole, not in bits and pieces. A *Brahman* Social Justice Department secretary may be the Nodal Officer for Atrocities Act and an SC/ST *devaswam* officer may be responsible for the welfare of the *Brahman pujari*s in the temple. Thus, the SC/ST employee is in the government neither for his own welfare nor even of his community. The government as a whole is responsible for the wellbeing (not welfare) of people as a whole. Reservation ensures share in the government (representation).

Only parents do not constitute social; they do not even constitute fully the family

Creamy layer is to be decided on the basis of socio-economic position of the parents. The term social is not encompassed by only parents but the wider group. If someone is forward or backward solely because of the parents then the right word for it is 'parental' or 'family backwardness'. An individual's socio-economic position is the function of not just his parents and grandparents but his extended relation and even his/her community. That the law cannot handle it does not mean this reality vanishes in the air. Regarding the limitation of law to handle untouchability, Ambedkar said—'law cannot punish an entire society or deal with societal "organised conspiracy". Even in law, in the Hindu Undivided Family and the *mitakshara* inheritance system, somebody's status is not determined only by their parents but by a wider circle. The social status of a group sometimes is dependent on some mythical ancestor who might have done or undone something.

Conclusion

Manu said:

> No *Shudra* should have property of his own, He should have nothing of his own. The existence of a wealthy *Shudra* is bad for the *Brahmans*. A *Brahman* may take possession of the goods of a *Shudra*.

I think the insistence of creamy layer by upper castes is jealousy (psychological) and worry about losing power (sociological). This is natural.

NOTES

1. *Round Table India,* 5 October, 2018. http://roundtableindia.co.in/index.php?option=com_content&view=article&id=9478:creamy-layer-jurisprudence-in-the-air&catid=119:feature&Itemid=132.
2. Rajagopal, Krishnadas, "In a first, plea in apex court seeks SC/ST creamy layer's exclusion from quota", *The Hindu*, January 28, 2018.

10

Fifty per cent Ceiling on Reservation: Can Efficiency Override Justice?[1]

The supreme court has fixed fifty per cent as the limit of reservation. It hasn't enlightened the populace about the rationale and the jurisprudential principle involved in it. While there are academic acrobatics around reservation and creamy layer there is no deliberation around this. It appears that the logic of 50 per cent ceiling on reservation is made up of titanium.

The principle seems to be the principle of equality—50 per cent unreserved vis-à-vis 50 per cent reserved. The 50:50 division is based on the principle of formal equality. But this leads to a strange situation. Out of hundred, 50 per cent reserved category is based on the principle of substantive equality while the other 50 per cent is based on formal equality. This is a situation where formal equality and substantive equality are given equal weight. But usually substantive equality is supposed to be better than formal equality and override formal equality. That's how first of all 50 per cent reservation can be given.

If substantive equality is applied throughout the hundred per cent then there is no violation of the principle of equality. Substantive equality applied to the entire 100 per cent means pro rata representation of all clusters of groups like the Scheduled Castes and Scheduled Tribes. However, the court definitely is against such arrangement and its opinion is that fifty per cent should be free from reservation. This means that the 50 per cent reservation free sphere is based not on the principle of equality but some other principle. That other principle must be efficiency.

Once we assume that the 50 per cent reservation free space is based on the principle of efficiency then the whole arrangement becomes not an exercise of the principle of equality but the principle of proportionality. It involves balancing justice (50 per cent reserved category) vis-à-vis efficiency (the 50 per cent general category). Once it is formulated like this it's a bit easier to comment on the proportion of the pie that should be reservation free.

When we utter that something is a balance of two principles (justice and efficiency) obviously it reminds oneself of John Rawls because his concern was also to balance two principles. He balanced it by making the 'difference principle' subservient to the 'equality principle'. His first principle can be seen as substantive equality because without this there cannot be 'equal liberty'. Rawls's equality is so severe that he is not willing to give anything extra to the individual for his or her natural talent because he considers them as simply accident. This clearly implies the subservience of efficiency to equality and therefore justice. He will subject the efficiency to the equality principle rather than the other way round. Efficiency can find a place in his difference principle which is subservient to the first principle.

Justice literature tells us that justice is the ultimate virtue and overrides any other concerns. That justice overrides efficiency will be evident from the kind of questions which we can ask to justice and efficiency. We can ask 'efficiency for what' but we cannot ask 'justice for what'. We can trade off efficiency for justice but not vice versa. A dictatorship can be efficient but not just.

Once we settle that justice overrides efficiency and both are not of equal worth, instinctively we can figure out that the sphere of efficiency must be smaller than the sphere of justice. If the sphere of efficiency is not smaller than justice then there is a chance of efficiency trampling down justice. But if we are convinced that justice overrides efficiency then why do we even need efficiency! Why not the hundred per cent be based just on the basis of justice? Instinctively we feel that this cannot be because justice itself needs efficiency and efficiency also needs justice. The need of efficiency is illustrated in the saying 'justice delayed is justice denied'. This statement illustrates that efficiency is a component in justice. The same compensation received in time is justice and received after much delay is injustice. However, it is common sense that only efficiency is not justice. There is also the saying that let justice be done even if the world collapses. This means justice is not expediency and quick fixes. It is the right thing at the right time. You not only want the justice quickly but you also want that ultimately what you get looks like justice and not something else. This is the qualitative aspect of justice and efficiency cannot compensate for it. The qualitative aspect of justice is best illustrated by Eugen Ehrlich's statement that 'there is no such thing as one justice only, as there is no such thing as one beauty only'. This is the reason why justice (phenomenology) has to triumph over efficiency (positivism).

Sometimes we don't have to even trade efficiency for justice as both may converge. Ambedkar said that most of the workers of Gandhi's *Harijan Sevak Sangh* should be untouchables as they will be interested in improving the condition of the untouchable. If the department of social justice which works for SC/ST consists mostly of SC/ST then there is a convergence of efficiency as well as justice because appointing of such persons itself is an act of justice. Justice has many facets—social, political, economic. Without political justice other justices are vulnerable. Reservation in government is more about political and social justice and not economic justice.

Once we agree that efficiency is necessary but subservient to justice then what is left for us is to decide the sphere of efficiency which instinctively, we know has to be smaller than justice. The only problem is how small the sphere of efficiency must be. It has to be of such proportion that its contribution to the society is much more compared to the price society pays for it in terms of waiving the social justice requirement. Applying Rawls to the Indian context justice can give in to efficiency if the end result is beneficial to the marginalised. Empirically, this involves running a 'justice audit' on any particular institution like the IIT. It means posing the question what IITs have taken from the Indian society and what they have given in return which has benefited the mass at the bottom. In a hypothetical case, the difference principle is applied when the state waives the requirement of reservation to a technical institute which in turn produces the technology which obviates the need of manual scavenging and the need for human labour in the sewers. This is a hypothetical example as such exercise (justice audit) has not been done by the academia in India.

After this travel, we come to the supreme court judgement where it says that reservation cannot be applied to speciality and super speciality. That sphere is to be reservation free which is in the nature of speciality and super speciality. Speciality and super speciality has to be a small percentage. It cannot be a humongous 50 per cent making the idea of speciality and super speciality ridiculous. Most part and level of the government cannot claim to be speciality and super speciality.

Conclusion

The fifty per cent threshold makes sense only when it is seen as an application of the principle of formal equality. It loses its sanctity if the arrangement is seen as an application of the principle of proportionality where one weighs the comparative weights of justice with efficiency.

NOTE

1. *Round Table India*, 12 October 2018. http://roundtableindia.co.in/index.php?option=com_content&view=article&id=9485:50-ceiling-on-reservation-can-efficiency-override-justice&catid=119:feature&Itemid=132

11

Questioning Excellence: Expelling 73 Students in IIT Roorkee[1]

The Indian Institute of Technology (IIT) Roorkee had expelled 73 students for under performance, of which 90 per cent belonged to reserved categories. Later they were allowed to take a re-examination following the Uttarakhand High Court's order. The initial move by the IIT cannot be restricted to the single act of expulsion from an institution of higher education—it has wider ramifications. This act can be replicated by any other educational institution, in any other sphere. The question that needs to be asked is this—can one take away in the name of autonomy/merit what one enables by way of social justice?

Reservation and Merit

There are two ways to understand Scheduled Caste and Scheduled Tribe (SC/ST) reservation in educational institutions. According to one argument the resources (seats in educational institution) belong to society at large and society can dispose of it in the fairest way possible. SC/ST students are constituents of society and therefore historical wrongs are being corrected by providing means to affordable higher education. Exclusive merit argument is not applicable in this case.

The other way reservation of SC/ST can be understood in India is in terms of inter-generational restorative justice (Goldman 1979). According to this, if the principle of justice is violated at one time it has to be restored subsequently, otherwise justice has no meaning. Subsequent generation can be recompensed on behalf of the generation which was wronged because the wronged generation is dead. The resource to recompense comes from society at large which was originally responsible for the widespread discrimination in the first place.

All these arguments are now somewhat settled, framed by the constitution and formalised by the state. Upholders of the "so called merit" argument therefore tend to agree on this one time "concession." However, what proponents of merit propose is that once admitted, the SC/ST students have to conform to the "general yardstick."

Institutions and Autonomy

The issue of "general yardstick" and autonomy is integrally linked. One can draw fruitfully from the debate on particular professions and autonomy in this regard. Professions are granted autonomy on the premise that "they know best" (for you). Similarly, universities are to be given autonomy because they know best (for society).

However, Larson (1977) points out that autonomy should be distinguished from sovereignty. Autonomy is a tacit agreement between the profession and society. Society grants autonomy to the profession in good faith that the profession will not misuse autonomy. The abuse of autonomy is purported to be checked by a "code of conduct."

Autonomy and "code of conduct" does not prevent abuse—for example, doctors are accused of professional malpractice with alarming regularity and can be booked under the consumer protection act. Similarly, universities/academic institutions are to be granted autonomy on the premise that they know best, but there could be exceptions there as well. Thus, opinion is divided on the limits of this autonomy and the juncture at which governments should step in to address problems in these institutions.

Autonomy implies discretion which is a double-edged sword—it can do both good and bad. There is no autonomy if ends and means are highly defined. Luckily ends and means in educational organisations do not follow bureaucratic diktats.

It is in this kind of a situation that discrimination can masquerade as discretion. First, what is the ideal level of quality bench mark to be maintained? A particular benchmark requires removal of 73 students. Move the benchmark a little higher; it will require more students to be excluded. This begs the question at what level 24 carat *shuddha* (pure) merit will be attained. And, if these 73 students were not removed, how it would have affected the pursuit of quality by others?

Excellence for All

If we assume the IIT entrance examination and subsequent education in IIT as a coherent two-part system, then the reserved categories necessarily require additional support in the second part of the system after their entry into the first part of the system.

However, the discrimination continues there with arguments put forth like—why should IITs subsidise what could be interpreted as the fallout of a broken secondary school education system? The secondary education in turn will blame the primary education. In primary education a significant portion of the blame will be on social cultural capital or the divine who created such castes.

Elite institutions like IITs are ideally positioned to cater to a third-generation higher education participant rather than a first-generation learner. Thus, when a first generation enters these institutions, s/he faces an uphill task. An inability to communicate in English or poor skills in their chosen subjects is only a part of the problem.

It is best to illustrate this with the case of a *Dalit* student, studying for a masters degree in science at an IIT, to speculate what can work and why. The student failed in a course on "programming with C language" that was common to BTech and MSc. The remedial class was not necessarily a forum for strengthening concepts in the coursework, it was relegated to be an inferior version of the regular class by design—an

MTech teaching assistant, rather than a full-fledged professor, was teaching a class of 50. Fortunately, the student had an MTech roommate who made the effort to help him because both belonged to the same state. Thus, mentoring, which is more effective, has its sociological dimensions.

Institutions should look into their curricula and supporting structures when large numbers of students fail. The fault also lies with the way teacher-student relationships in higher education are established. This is not just an academic transaction, it has several socioeconomic factors working for as well as against it.

Islands of Excellence

Institutes of "national" importance should not feel burdened by national imperatives that are guided by the concerns of the privileged. If these islands of excellence are subsidised by the state, and in turn by society—often dubbed by neoliberals as the privatisation of public resources—then their actions cannot be beyond scrutiny.

IITs have not achieved their eminent position in India endogenously. They were designed from the start to be a class apart—perhaps even to exclude several others. Fine-tuning their teaching and research programmes to the developmental needs of a country steeped in discrimination is the need of the hour. Therefore, the question of whether merit can be defined by the circumstantially lucky few needs to be asked again and again.

NOTE

1. *Economic & Political Weekly,* L, No. 33, 15 August, 2015, web exclusive, https://www.epw.in/journal/2015/33/web-exclusives/questioning-excellence.html

REFERENCES

Larson, M.S., *The Rise of Professionalism: A Sociological Analysis.* London: University of California Press, 1977.

Goldman, A.H., *Justice and Reverse Discrimination.* New Jersey: Princeton University Press,1979.

12

Judicial Independence or Sovereignty![1]

Recently four judges of the collegium in the Supreme Court accused the chief justice of misuse of his discretion.[2] In this context, Upendra Baxi quotes the Austrian jurist Eugene Ehrlich—'the best guarantee of justice lies in the personality of the judge'[3]. It's not difficult to imagine what he is fending off. It is a bit puzzling when I am told that I am in a problem but cannot intervene to fix it. The key issue is judicial independence as against outside interference. One of the major points of intervention is appointments to the higher judiciary. In that, probably the most important issue is reservation/representation in the judiciary.

Are we interested in independence or impartiality?

Judicial independence cannot be like the independence of a country which means sovereignty of that country. Even sovereignty of a state in this age of globalisation is circumscribed by various international frameworks and realpolitik. Therefore, judicial independence can only mean 'independence in its own sphere'. But this type of independence is required not only for the judiciary but for every organ of the state. The executive too requires independence from judicial interference. The doctrine of proportionality applies to all the three branches. The three branches are based on the principle of separation of powers. But Max Weber distinguishes between limitations of power and separation of powers. 'Limitation of power exists; where, due to sacred tradition or enactment, a particular imperium is restrained by the rights of its subjects' (1978, 652). This means that there might be a zone of discretion within a particular sphere not restrained by separation of powers. The Roster in the court is probably such an instance.

Independence per se is not a virtue

Let's begin with a quote from the same Eugene Ehrlich.

> 'The judge has often, it is true, disregarded the law in the service of an unscrupulous sovereign power; occasionally, supported by law, he has been able to offer successful resistance to a strong sovereign power; but he has never risked a combat with the state, society, and traditional law. Much less has juristic science, with its limited powers, ever done this' (2002, 181).

No one is more independent than the despot. If this can be avoided by claiming oneself as a saviour then it sounds like a White Knight argument. If the White Knight argument is extended, it can support all oppression as every oppressor will say s/he is actually a saviour. That's why a good government cannot be a substitute for self-government. This indicates that what we really are interested in is impartiality rather than independence per se. Independence is supposed to be a requirement for impartiality and rightfully so. If a judge can be influenced from outside through various devices then obviously s/he has little scope for impartiality.

'Fairness', which implies impartiality, is the stuff of political theory. Amartya Sen (2010) prefers a 'comparative-actual behavioural' approach to that of a 'transcendental-institutional' approach (John Rawls). He prefers 'open impartiality' ('impartial spectator' of Adam Smith) to that of 'closed impartiality' (veil of ignorance of Rawls). The first type of impartiality assumes full information while the other an artificial suspending of all information. In case of Indian higher judiciary, the assumption seems to be the 'veil of ignorance' as bias is assumed away.

The debate on 'objectivity' in social science is like the debate on impartiality—to remove bias. Here, we have moved a long way from a scientific positivistic objectivity to an objectivity acquired through inter-subjective agreement. An 'inter-subjective' objectivity will be far away from the Rawlsian veil of ignorance.

External and internal independence

Independence is of two types—external and internal. External independence, of course, is attained through preventing external interference. But independence also means to be free from internal interference—the biases. The judge not only has to be free externally but also internally, in his mind, from biases. Justice Dowsett explores this in his paper (Dowsett 2010). According to him following are the ways in which biases can creep in unconsciously:

- Flowing from the theory of probability—if there are 10 domestic violence cases and 8 false, then the probability of the 11th case as false can create prejudice. This is before even the case has begun.
- Judge's opinion of a lawyer.
- Judge may not like particular type of cases.
- 'At trial, there are other potential sources of prejudice. Some are obvious—the witness who is, in one sense or another, attractive or unattractive; counsel who is co-operative, quick and well-prepared and counsel who is not; the case that is straightforward, and the case that resists all efforts to simplify it, or to reduce it to easily manageable proportions; the case that clearly merits the time, money and effort put into it, and the case that does not. Another possible source of prejudice is a premature conclusion as to the merits of the case. Prejudice may arise out of conflict between the case in hand and the judge's other commitments. This is a long-standing problem. As Pope wrote: Wretches hang that jurymen may dine' (ibid, 10).
- 'We may say "Let justice be done though the heavens fall", but there is, usually, an understandable desire to

> avoid such a catastrophe. On the other hand, it must be acknowledged that some people revel in producing startling effects. This, too, can be a source of judicial prejudice'(ibid, 10-11).

This independence of mind is not fixed but can change. Justice Bhagwati, Beg, and Chandrachud, who were in Maneka Gandhi case, also were in the majority side in ADM Jabalpur case. This may point out that they exercised their independence in Maneka Gandhi case which they did not in the case of ADM Jabalpur. This shows that a positivistic conception of permanent objectivity is more of a theoretical construct. The complaint of the four judges against the Chief Justice (CJ) seems to be that the CJ is abusing his discretion. Such abuse cannot be prevented by a rule-based positivistic objectivity. What the four are really pointing at is an objectivity in the sense of inter-subjective agreement. But, if we really want to attain inter-subjective objectivity, then the representation of all sections of society is necessary. When upper caste judges decide about reservation issue, there is a possibility of a conflict of interest. Simply invoking a 'veil of ignorance' won't produce one.

Does legislative participation in appointment take away the independence? External independence is attained not only through appointment but also by making removal difficult. In spite of the collegium, the parliament still has the power to impeach. Should it want to abuse that power, collegium won't be able to prevent that.

If court makes law, then it cannot avoid the question of representation

Hardly anybody will dispute on 'no taxation (legislation) without representation'. A non- representative body ought not make laws in a democracy. This is the logic of representation in parliament and the nitty-gritty (reservation) thereof. Representation in judiciary is really not warranted if it is merely an interpreter or umpire. But it is widely agreed that courts not only interpret law, but also make laws. Justice Oliver

Wendell Holmes said 'the prophecies of what the courts will do in fact and nothing more pretentious are what I mean by Law' (Ratnapala 2009). The position of the Realist jurisprudence is that 'law is what the court says'. In the Indian context there are many rights—health, education, water, pollution free air etc.—which have been created by the Supreme Court. So, to say that courts merely interpret and not create law, is a bit of a rhetorical statement. The clever way of saying the same is that court 'finds' the law. Max Weber has said that both law making and law finding can be both rational and irrational. 'Lawmaking and law finding are substantively irrational to the extent that decision is influenced by facts of the particular case as evaluated upon an ethical, emotional, or political basis rather than by general norms' (1978, 656). 'As late a writer as Blackstone called the English judge a sort of living oracle' (ibid, 767). In the contemporary times Justice Aharon Barak in his book commented:

> the main issue is, of course, how should we determine the social importance of the benefits gained by the limiting law and the social importance of preventing harm to the limited constitutional right. The answer is that the determination is not scientific or accurate. The balancing between conflicting principles is not conducted through scientific instruments. Rather, it is derived, inter alia, from different political and economic ideologies, from the unique history of each country, from the structure of the political system, and from different social values (Barak 2012, 349).

This basically means that there is nothing like a standalone objectivity. Justice is a balancing act. Independence has to be balanced against impartiality. The 'independence' theory is based on the assumption that judges do not create fact but only apply laws to the fact. Fact is yours and law is yours. Therefore, all that is done is applying a law to the fact. Therefore, you do not need representation. However, law can make facts in the common sensical notion relevant or irrelevant (the admissible and inadmissible evidence), can create new facts like the juristic personality. According to Ehrlich, it is impossible to separate the question of fact from the question of law. ' ... in the language of jurists, in a much greater number of instances, judgement is being rendered upon questions of fact than upon questions of law' (Ehrlich 2002, 35).

Statistical proof is used to capture indirect discrimination

'Numbers do not lie' is a bit extreme position. But they must be given a hearing. Numbers lead to profound results. The starting point of Weber's *Protestant Ethic and Spirit of Capitalism* was statistics. Weber proceeded from an empirical study of one of his pupils, Martin Offenbacher, on occupational stratification according to religious denominations in Baden. It revealed that a disproportionate number of Protestants owned capital and entrepreneurs and made up the higher qualified technical or sales personnel in the business. Then he collected similar studies about towns especially of 16th century to see if any relationship between certain expressions of the old Protestant spirit and modern capitalistic culture is to be found (Kasler 1988). The result was a widely influential book. One could see what the initial statistics led to.

In the legal sphere, proof by the statistical test is an evidentiary device to capture indirect discrimination. Legal architecture, including statistical proof, to counter indirect discrimination is already in place in EU and UK. With due respect to the court, the fact of the extremely low percentage of SC/ST in the higher judiciary (Prasanna Kumar 2016), if it was in a government department, would have been a fitting case of indirect discrimination, if there was a law on indirect discrimination with provision for statistical proof.

Conclusion

George Gadbois Jr, for readers' ease, tells in a stylized manner about judges of the Supreme Court of India in the chapter called *The Archetypal Judge* in his book:

He was the son of a lawyer, often born into a family where the practice of law had been a tradition for generations. He was a Hindu and, more likely than not, a *Brahman*. He was born in an urban area into a wealthy or upper-middle-class family...He may have met the usual criteria of merit-integrity, professional competence, incorruptibility, and neutrality towards litigants—but was not selected for that reason. His religion, seniority, state, and region of origin, among other considerations, were more weighty than merit as traditionally defined....He remained active after leaving the bench. Serving on officially appointed commissions or tribunals and chamber practice were the most common post-retirement activities (2011, 376-377).

NOTES

1. *Round Table India*, 22 January, 2018, http://roundtableindia.co.in/index.php?option=com_content&view=article&id=9280:judicial-independence-or-sovereignty&catid=119:feature&Itemid=132.
2. https://timesofindia.indiatimes.com/india/live-updates-unprecedented-press-conference-by-4-senior-sc-judges/articleshow/62470543.cms Accessed on January 12, 2018.
3. Upendra Baxi, "When judges dissent", *The Indian Express*, January 18, 2018.

REFERENCES

Barak, Aharon, *Proportionality: Constitutional Rights and their Limitations*. Cambridge: Cambridge University Press, 2012.

Dowsett, J.A., 'Prejudice—The Judicial Virus'. *Australian Journal of Forensic Sciences* 42, No. 1 (2010): 37-48.

Ehrlich, Eugen, *Fundamental Principles of the Sociology of Law*. London: Transaction Publishers, 2002.

Gadbois, Jr, George H., *Judges of the Supreme Court of India 1950-1989*. Delhi: Oxford University Press, 2011.

Kasler, Dirk, *Max Weber: An Introduction to His Life and Work*. UK: Polity Press,1988.

Alok, Prasanna Kumar, 'Absence of Diversity in the Higher Judiciary'. *Economic & Political Weekly*, LI, No. 8 (2016): 10-11.

Sen, Amartya, *The Idea of Justice*. UK: Penguin, 2010.

Weber, Max, *Economy and Society—an Outline of Interpretive Sociology*, University of California Press, 1978. https: / / archive,org / stream / MaxWeberEconomyAndSociety / MaxWeberEconomyAndSociety_ djvu,txt Accessed on April 15, 2016.

13

Reservation in Private Sector Employment: Is It Justified?[1]

Reservation in private for-profit sector is advocated on two grounds (1) that there is discrimination; (2) and they have a social obligation. The counter argument against (1) is that there is no incentive for discrimination for a business since it is concerned only with money—so only with merit. If business avoids merit, it will dig its own grave. The counter argument to this counter argument is that there is both business compulsion and personal imperative to do discrimination. Against (2) the counter argument is that the 'private' is protected by autonomy absolving it of social obligation. The counter argument to this is that the supposed claim of the autonomy of the private is based on mixing up the 'private' with the 'personal' and 'autonomy' with 'license'. This paper holds that the main reason of all these obfuscations is due to a 'binary' view rather than a 'continuum' view. The paper will apply a 'continuum' view throughout and arrive at a middle ground between 'reservation' and 'affirmative action' in the private sector.

It is the question of reservation in business/corporate sector employment that raises maximum heat but little light. State intervention in private sector education is nothing new in India. The Supreme Court has upheld the RTE mandated 25 per cent reservation in private schools.[2] The private non-profit sector, popularly known as the NGO sector, has the latitude to be arbitrary. But they accept social responsibility ab initio.[3] Thus, some of them may be working entirely for the marginalised most of whom are Scheduled Caste and Scheduled Tribe. Thus, the issue of discrimination does not arise so much theoretically and therefore reservation. Nobody disputes the justification of regulation of functioning of private non-profit and for-profit sector. However, it is reservation in the private for-profit sector employment (business/the corporate sector) that raises maximum theoretical challenge and practical hostility because of the supposed sanctity of autonomy of the private sphere in a liberal regime. This creates a theoretical quagmire of sort whereby people do not dispute the regulation of functioning of private sector but strongly resist any idea of reservation in the business/corporate sector at the same time. To get out of this quagmire, this paper will take help mainly from three books—Thorat, Aryama and Negi (2007); Khaitan (2015); Mahajan and Reifeld (2003).

Thorat, Aryama and Negi (2007) tries to defend reservation in the private sector. However, it does not demolish the myth of the inviolability of the 'private' which is necessary to defend reservation in the 'private' sector. This is done by Mahajan and Reifeld (2003), which demolishes the myth of the inviolability and innocence of the 'private'. Tarunabh Khaitan's (2015) theoretical elaboration of anti-discrimination laws paves the way for it as a theoretical defence of reservation in the private sector. Apart from taking help of the three books the paper will justify reservation by applying a 'continuum' instead of a binary view to 'public-private'. Zadeh (1988) argues that in fuzzy logic, in contrast to crispy logic, everything, including truth, is a matter of degree and should be regarded as a continuum (cited in Chalabi 2014, 133). An adversarial dichotomous view employs pairs like real-ideal, subjective-objective, theory-practice, qualitative-quantitative, etc. In contrast, a 'continuum' view views that reality is not black and white but with a shade of gray. For example, it has taken a long time for the society to accept that there is a third gender apart from male and female.

There are three ways the continuum view can help us to get us out of the deadlock on the debate on reservation in the private sector. First the public-private can be seen as a continuum rather than 'either-or'. The 'duellist' approach to the debate on reservation pits 'reservation' against 'merit', 'public' against 'private' as if both cannot co-exist at the same time. Second, discrimination also can be seen as a continuum from a very high to a very low degree. This can support the view that private sector has varied degrees of latitude to practise discrimination. This can also counter any notion that there cannot be discrimination in the public sector. Third, the continuum view also takes us out of an inflexible fixed reservation system based on population proportion as a solution to a dynamic flexible reservation system suitable for a vast and varied private sector.

(1) There is both business compulsion and personal imperative to do discrimination in business.

Khaitan (2015) agrees that past and current discrimination is the strongest ground to call for affirmative action. Current prevalent discrimination is the ground on which reservation in the private sector can be justified. Discrimination in the private sector is now brought out by empirical studies (Thorat, 2005). That's why, almost instinctively, the usual defence by the private sector against reservation is that they go only by merit and nothing else to obviate the charge of discrimination. It is then not surprising that they do not take cover under 'autonomy' of the private. However, let's take the merit argument and see if it is convincing. This has two parts. First, the private sector has no incentive for discrimination. Second, if it does, then it creates its own peril. The counter to this is that the private sector has both business and personal imperative to discriminate.

(1.1) Discrimination—the business imperative

> Remember that the professor, the teacher, is paid to be suspicious, skeptical, and argumentative. That's our job ... And so, when a

> businessman meets a professor, you can see the shutters go down over their eyes and their jaws tighten as each faces his mortal antagonist; the man whose life depends on accepting assumptions up against the man whose life depends on questioning them (Gurney cited in Thomas 1989, 24).

Business discriminates because it makes business sense. A simple definition of business is 'buying and selling'. For what? Only a moron can ask what the private for-profit sector is for! The first priority is to stay in the business. If the business questions social practices then it faces the risk of social hostility which will affect its business. The state is oriented to 'citizens' and 'persons' while the corporate sector is oriented to the 'customer'. Corporate sector does not question and rather make money from social evils like junk food, tobacco and alcohol products. Therefore, if discrimination exists in society, business is likely to follow it. A business would not like to alienate its existing upper caste employees or customers by hiring a lower caste.

(1.2) Discrimination—the personal imperative

The merit discourse assumes a rational businessman for whom monetary profit is everything. Max Weber's study *Protestant Ethic and Spirit of Capitalism* shows the link between a religious notion and capital formation by making money systematically. The notion in question is 'predestination', much like the notion of karma. This is not something rational. We can legitimately go further and raise the suspicion that whether a businessman will be influenced by only one part of the religion and no other parts. It is useful to remember that our value system remains as a package rather than neat categories like social or religious values. Values can influence how to earn and how to spend. This is exemplified by the spending of two industrialists—Vijay Mallya and Azim Premji. While one chose to spend away, the other chose to give away. This may or may not speak about their religious differences but certainly their value differences. From here, it is not difficult to imagine that religious and other values can influence who to recruit, how to recruit and how to treat the employees. All this shows that if a businessman is like any other fallible mortal, s/he can discriminate. If corporate sector can do financial crime, environmental crime, then why cannot they do discrimination!

(2) The extent of discrimination possible

Corporate sector's second defence could be that even if they wish, they will dig their own grave if they discriminate and not go by merit. If we apply the continuum view, discrimination can be to various degrees. It looks plausible that a corporation will collapse if it does not bother about merit on a large scale. However, most have an elbow room. Bigger the size, wider the elbow room. This elbow room arises because of two reasons.

(2.1) To the extent of the fuzziness of the concept of merit

The private sector has simply asserted away that they go by merit. They have not proved it. Neither they can, because of the lack of a consensus on the definition of merit and how to spot it. How do you spot leadership in two or three interviews! There is recognition in social science of the effect of 'affect'. Generally, there are four biases that can creep in an interview—effects of the interviewer, interviewee, latent identity and the situation (Hammersely and Atkinson 1983). The latent identity effects are ascribed features like looks, caste etc. that are difficult to hide. If the sage Vishwamitra could be distracted, how can ordinary mortals remain unbiased!

If personnel merit is the only crucial factor then public sector should not be making profit and private sector should not be making losses. That brings into the picture a host of other issues like 'risk', 'government policy', 'macro environment' etc. When it comes to reservation, private sector defends itself with merit, but in other times it discusses market, external environment, policy etc. Whether a meritorious person can triumph over hostile environment is not discussed logically.

(2.2) To the extent of the limit of law

The extent of discrimination possible for the corporates also arises out of the limit of law. Discrimination is prohibited by law. However, the law has its limit, sometimes in pure quantitative terms. The CBI stated before the supreme court that it simply does not have the manpower to investigate DMAT scam.[4] The law cannot investigate massive private sector recruitment to check for discrimination. Theoretically, the margin of discrimination is proportionate to the limits of law which can be quantitative (manpower) and qualitative (to prove indirect discrimination). If a law on indirect discrimination with provision for validity of statistical test comes into being in India, then the net effect for the private sector would be to either prove non-discrimination or take affirmative action.

(3) Reservation for upper caste does exist in the private sector—the notions of *de jure/de facto* and formal/substantive

It is fashionable to claim that there is no reservation in the private sector. Similarly, it is fashionable to claim that reserved category people get extra chance as they have access to the so called 'general'/'open category' in addition to the reserved category. However, SC/ST instinctively feel that the so called open category is actually not open to them. Phenomenology suggests that they might have a point. What really happens is that the so called 'open category' is open to all just like a five star hotel is open to all. It is obvious that a five star is formally open to all but practically reserved for the rich. Similarly, there is no way that most reserved category students can compete in the open category because of a lack of a level playing field.

The notions of *de jure* vs *de facto* and formal vs substantive are widely used in social sciences. The terms are used in many contexts. Political science uses *de jure* and *de facto* sovereignty. Justice literature distinguishes between formal and substantive justice. Béteille has underscored the difference between formal and substantive citizenship in India:

> What took two hundred years and more in the West was accomplished overnight in India where subjects were transformed into citizens with the adoption of a republican constitution. But while all Indians are in a purely formal sense citizens under its constitution the public in any politically meaningful sense of the term is still highly restricted. The disabilities of subjecthood have been removed, but the abilities essential for effective citizenship have not been created (Béteille 2003, 49-50).

If we apply the notions of *de jure/de facto* and formal/substantive then we can guess that though the private sector can claim to be formally open to all, there will be *de facto* reservations for upper castes/classes if they are already dominant in them. The upper class-caste fills up the upper echelons of the private sector. It is unlikely that their children will not find a place in the private sector. Thus, there is a high chance that the private sector is *de facto* reserved for upper caste-class if they are already dominant there.

(4) The private sphere is not to be found at one end of the public-private continuum but has to be deduced from the public

One of the major defences against reservation in the private sector is the supposed autonomy and inviolability of the 'private'. But confusion happens when one takes a binary view of social phenomenon that is in reality a continuum. If we make an epistemological push on the public-private distinction it will look like the following.

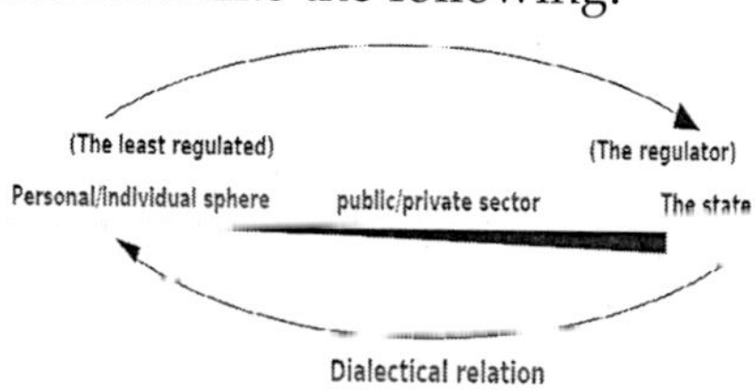

Figure 12.1: The Personal-Public/Private-Government Continuum

The varied meanings of 'private' can justify the above continuum. 'There is private in the sense of the personal...

sexual... family or household' (Uberoi 2003, 206-207). Underscoring the dialectical relation between the state and the individual points out that what is private in the sense of personal (to be least regulated) does not remain fixed but changes with the times. This means whatever the meaning of private—personal, sexual, family or household—it does not get absolved from public regulation. Terms like 'private law' and 'personal law' in India indicate that regulation can get into the 'private' or 'personal'. 'Whether a person should 'smoke' tobacco is as much a private choice as well as a public concern. 'Private' concerns and choices are often portrayed by legislation or judicial interpretation as public wrongs. This dilutes legal distinction between 'public' and 'private' aspects of law' (Dhavan 2003, 162). The Supreme Court in *Murli S. Deora vs. Union of India and Ors*[5] has held that smoking in public affects non-smokers' right to life (Article 21 of the constitution).

Does it mean the personal is/should open to public regulation to the same degree as the public-private? Instinctively we feel that it should not. We can state that the personal should have *least* regulation but not *no regulation.*

> We no longer consider it just to coerce a labourer or a prostitute to serve anyone willing to pay, even if they held themselves out as a common labourer or a common prostitute. Given the deeply personal nature of the 'service' they provide, the cost of such coercion to their negative liberty will be too large (Khaitan 2015, 206).

> ...as long as people choose between alternatives acceptable to society—in other words, as long as they do not break the rules of what is not acceptable—an individual's privacy cannot be transgressed upon. But if individuals are found to break the rules—at home, in the garden, or on the streets—the public will intervene (Gupta 2003, 70).

In the middle of the continuum we have a sphere that can be simultaneously private and public to various degrees. We already have seen that smoking is simultaneously a personal as well as public act. Similarly, the corporate sector operates in the public sphere. Acts are public to the extent they affect others as members of public. *Most of the acts of private corporate like recruitment are to be regulated not because they are private but because they are public acts.* While private acts can be personal preference based public acts have to be based on public imperative. One of the most important imperatives of the public sphere is equality—both formal and substantive. The autonomy of the private is problematic because the definition of private itself cannot be private but public. Otherwise rule of law will be infructuous as any wrongdoing will be claimed as 'private'. Laws on indirect discrimination are nothing but a check on misuse of autonomy.

If we take a 'continuum' view, reservation need not drive out merit, public need not drive out private. Public-private are not dichotomous. The difference between a public sector and a private sector can be sometimes literally 2 per cent,—when the government stake can be 51 per cent and the private 49 per cent in a particular entity. Again, if we take a continuum view, the private can range from a one man shop to an MNC (Multi National Corporation) having lakhs of employees. The private also includes the 'for-profit' and 'non-profit' sector. The non-profit sector projects that they believe in an ideology of social justice, and merit is not an issue to them. However, many NGOs (Non-Government Organisations) are yet to recognize caste. While they mention openly that they will prefer a female with similar qualification to that of a male, they are yet to mention such a thing about caste.

These arguments, while apparently solving the puzzle of the justification of the regulation of the private sector employment—through establishing that it is actually a public act—also creates another puzzle—what is private or what part of the private that cannot be touched? If we obliterate private, we won't be any longer in liberalism. The solution lies in deducing the private from the public. The private itself cannot be defined privately but has to be defined publicly.

When an industrialist transfers his wealth to his son, the act/consequence is private but the procedure of establishing this is public. If 'inheritance tax' is applied, greater public content is assumed; if not, lesser. The supreme private act is the appropriation of profit. But the definition of profit to be appropriated is a public one. There cannot be any relaxations on various standards like environment, labour, product and various taxes, though all of it impacts the profit. On the other hand, public acts invite charges of corruption to the extent they are private acts. All these show that a single act is private and public to various extents.

(5) Changing social contract changes respective obligations

Khaitan's (2015) position is that a universalistic solution is better than a particularistic solution like reservation which antagonizes the cognate group which does not get the reservation. This he calls as the 'expressive cost'. His view is that only when universalistic solution is not feasible then particularistic solutions like affirmative action/reservation should be favoured. However, he does not take the argument to its logical conclusion. Universalistic measures are provided only under socialism. Reservation can happen only in a liberal regime. The question of reservation does not arise in socialist regime because society starts from a clean slate in a socialist regime (Goldman 1979). A socialist paradigm does not consider 'private' (especially property) deserving protection. That's how land reforms and nationalisation of banks in India could be justified. However, this seems unthinkable in the present neo-liberal era. Therefore, a liberal framework which does not prevent the inherited advantages of some, has to give a certain level playing field to some others who are thus disadvantaged ab initio.

Since reservation is an eminent liberal concern, reservation in the private sector has to be justified from a contractarian point of view which is the justificatory paradigm of a liberal regime. The heuristic purpose is best served by seeing the contract as dynamic. From a contractarian point of view, 'public' and 'private' come into being consequent to a decision to that effect. This is reflected in industrial policies which earmark public and private spheres for economic activities. The changing social contract is evident by the fact that the Indian state and society accepts a much bigger diameter of the private sphere today. It is not that this bigger private sphere is averse to say how public they are. They are proud of their CSR. When a big company proudly talks about its contribution to the country's GDP, it intends not to show how private it is but how public it is, how society wide is its presence. Add up some of the big companies and one gets a rough idea about the economy or even the society. They influence substantially the polity, economy and society. If still they are called private, it's an analytical distinction and not substantive—just like sometimes the government behaves like the agent of some companies.

> powerful private interests control governance—both directly or indirectly or through a systemic use of the process of governance... the more we know about the real working of government the more we realize how tenuous the distinction between the 'private' and 'public' domain is in real life. The Vohra Committee Report (Government of India 1995) revealed the vast nexus between hoodlums and governance in India (Dhavan 2003, 160).

Often private sector performs public functions like running a hospital, educational institutions, providing electricity. Eventually they may gobble up most of the public functions. Even security, which was supposed to be a state preserve, is now privatised with increasing number of private security agencies. How can private gobble up public functions without assuming some of the public responsibilities! The 'New Public Management' expects the government sector to imbibe the virtues of the private sector. If public sector can be expected to imbibe the virtues of private sector like 'efficiency', why cannot private sector be expected to imbibe some of the supposed virtues of government sector like 'social justice'! One cannot only teach and not learn.

Conclusion—Between affirmation and reservation—between procedure based and outcome-based measures

While procedure-based measures will impact operational autonomy, outcome-based measures may appear harsh. Reservation will be result based evidence of non-discrimination. But imposing the quantum of population proportion is unrealistic, as government itself has not achieved this ideal. Therefore, while the population proportion remains the ideal, the benchmark, lower than this, could be linked to the size of the company or any other relevant criteria. The focus of an Equal Opportunities Commission will be on those who deviate too much from this ideal bench mark.

NOTES

1. *The Voice* 4, No. 2 (2017): 138-148.
2. Society for Unaided Private Schools of Rajasthan v Union of India & Another (2012) 6 SCC 1; Writ Petition (C) No. 95 of 2010.
3. For some of the differences between public, private for profit and non-profit sector, see Khora (2016, 150).
4. http://indianexpress.com/article/india/india-others/not-enough-manpower-to-probe-scam-bigger-than-vyapam-cbi-to-sc/#sthash.d76TYvrd.dpuf Accessed on June 20, 2017.
5. AIR 2002 SC 40, 2002 (1) ALD 88 SC, 2001 (6) ALT 35 SC (The Supreme Court of India) Available at http://indiankanoon.org/doc/1495522.

REFERENCES

Béteille, Andre', 'The Public as a Social Category'. Mahajan and Reifeld, 2003, pp. 37-55.

Chalabi, Azadeh, 'Law as a System of Rights: A Critical Perspective'. *Human Rights Review* 15 (2014): 117–138.

Dhavan, Rajeev, 'Law's Magic and Empire Revisited: Public Spaces and Private Lives—The Domain of the Law'. Mahajan and Reifeld, pp. 149-180.

Goldman, A.H., *Justice and Reverse Discrimination.* New Jersey: Princeton University Press, 1979.

Gupta, Dipankar, 'The Domesticated Public: Tradition, Modernity and the Public/Private Divide'. Mahajan and Reifeld, pp. 56-73.

Hammersely, Martin and Paul Atkinson, *Ethnography: Principles in Practice.* London & Newyork: Tavistock Publications,1983.

Khaitan, Tarunabh, *A Theory of Discrimination Law.* Delhi: Oxford University Press, 2015.

Khora, Sthabir, 'Education Management in India the Need For Caution'. *International Journal of Research in Economics and Social Sciences (IJRESS)* 6, No. 8 (2016): 133-152.

Mahajan, Gurpreet, Helmut Reifeld (eds.), *The Public and the Private: Issues of Democratic Citizenship.* New Delhi: Sage Publications, 2003.

Thomas, Alan B., 'One-Minute Management Education: A Sign of the Times?' *Management Learning* 20 (1989): 23-37.

Thorat, Sukhadeo, 'Reservation and Efficiency'. *Economic & Political Weekly* 40, No. 9 (2005): 808-810.

Thorat, Sukhdeo, Aryama and Prashant Negi (eds.), *Reservation and Private Sector: Quest for Equal Opportunity and Growth.* Jaipur: Rawat Publications, 2007.

Uberoi, Patricia, 'Feminism and the Public-Private Distinction'. Mahajan and Reifeld, pp. 205-228.

PART III

LAW, ATROCITY AND DISCRIMINATION

14

'Final Reports' Under Section 498A and the SC/ST Atrocities Act[1]

The failure by the police to file a First Information Report is the subject of much debate but the Final Report by which a case is closed has received scant attention. This article reflects on the findings following a study of 100 Final Reports each under Section 498A of the Indian Penal Code and the Scheduled Castes/Scheduled Tribes (Prevention of Atrocities) Act, 1989. The police's differential stance on these two laws has major implications in terms of justice delivery.

Popular perception understandably associates justice with the courts. The much quoted Bollywood dialogue *tarikh pe tarikh* (date upon date) depicts the endless delay of justice in the courts, but nevertheless portrays the court as the dispenser of justice. However, in reality, justice at the first instance is much more beholden to what the police say. Therefore, justifiably, there is a concern about the refusal or delay in filing the First Information Report (FIR). The television serial FIR is symbolic of people's awareness of this first step in the justice system which sets the process in motion. Two important indicators discussed in the academic as well as the popular discourse on justice are "incidence of crime" and "conviction rate". However, both these discourses do not focus much on the Final Report (FR) which is truly the first-line of justice/injustice delivery. It is almost a verdict by the police that the case does not deserve to go to the court. If oppression has indeed taken place, such a verdict by the police has serious implications for the delivery of justice. Not much public consternation is witnessed when a sizeable chunk of cases, sometimes amounting to 50 per cent in the case of the Scheduled Castes/Scheduled Tribes (Prevention of Atrocities) Act, 1989 (henceforth the SC/ST Act) and 498A of the Indian Penal Code (IPC) do not go to court. They result in the FR and are closed.

When an FIR is lodged, the police investigate and send it to the court (charge sheet) or close it because of mistakes of fact or law under Section 173 of the IPC. Theoretically, the superintendent of police (SP) sees the FR before it is submitted to the court, the court is supposed to inform the complainant, and the complainant has the option of a protest petition if s/he is not satisfied with the investigation. However, both the SP and the court, with their heavy workload, may not have so much time to take the preventive action of scrutinizing the FRs in detail from the point of view of law and fact before sanctioning it. That leaves a protest petition by the complainant as the only redress against a wrongful FR. But if the complainant is poor, illiterate and powerless before the social and politically powerful upper castes, how can s/he file a protest petition? Though s/he is supposed to know about the fate of his/her case, the information can always be stopped midway. Just like the dividend cheque of small shareholders which never seems to reach them or reaches very late, the notice may reach very late or be seized en route. It is the first-line/front line of justice/injustice. The complainant has two other options apart from the police station to lodge an FIR—the SP office and the court. But the FR is solely based on police investigation. Though the judiciary is not bound to accept the FR, it cannot appropriate the investigative function of the police. Therefore, the FR which is based on police investigation is very important.

Sociologically, women and members of the Scheduled Castes (SC)/Scheduled Tribes (ST) are considered to be part of the oppressed. Section 498A was inserted into the IPC in 1983 to provide a legal measure against domestic violence

(The Centre for Women Studies undated). The SC/ST Act, was enacted specifically as a legal redress mechanism to prevent atrocities motivated by caste (Saxena 2002). Periodically there is an uproar about the injustice due to the refusal or delay in filing an FIR and the very low rate of conviction in court under these laws. However, there is not as much focus in the popular and academic discourse on the large number of cases getting closed (FR) and not going to court. This is what the National Commission for Scheduled Castes (2004-05, 239) said:

> the central government and the state government should ensure that the underlying reasons for ending up the investigations in Final Report as acquittal of the accused is quite high in the states of Andhra Pradesh, Bihar, Rajasthan and UP, where maximum cases are registered under PCR and PoA Act, needs to be studied in depth.[2]

There were seven states in 2012 where more than 40 per cent cases under the SC/ST Act resulted in either "false"[3] or some other category of the FR.[4] There were four states in 2012 where between 40 per cent and 67 per cent cases and eight states where between 20 per cent and 40 per cent cases under Section 498A of the IPC resulted in either "false" or some other category of the FR out of the total cases investigated.[5]

Generally, the FR is also identified with "false" cases though it is one of the categories among others like "mistake of fact", "civil nature", etc. Occasionally, even the court expresses concern about the misuse of Section 498A and the SC/ST Act though one can argue that everything which has a "use" can also be misused. In this context, it becomes necessary to look at the FRs.

I have put down my reflections after studying 100 FRs each under these two laws in a state which has one of the highest rates of FRs.

Type of Final Report

The particular category under which an FR is labelled reflects the differential stance of the police towards 498A and the

SC/ST Act. While almost all the FRs under 498A are *galat fahmi* (wrong impression; legally "mistake of fact"), the overwhelming category of FRs under the SC/ST Act is "false". While "mistake of fact" does not invite any legal repercussions, "false" invites Sections 182 and 211 of the IPC. However, these sections are recommended in very few FRs. This could be due to the police not wanting to take on additional burden. There is a thin chance of success as the ex-complainant becomes the accused and avails of the "benefit of doubt". Falsity has to be proved beyond reasonable doubt. Nevertheless, using the label "false" and still not invoking Sections 182 and 211 of the IPC reflects the hostile attitude of the police towards the victims under the SC/ST Act. What could be the reason that the police predominantly label the FRs under the SC/ST Act as false while they could as well have labelled them mistake of fact like the FRs under Section 498A? The reason could very well be caste. While 498A is not caste specific, the SC/ST Act is especially meant for the lowest of castes.

Delay in Reporting and Veracity of the Case

Courts count the delay in reporting in hours and take a serious view if it is in days. While a delay of a few days in reporting is construed as lack of veracity with respect to the SC/ST Act, the same is not the situation in regard to complaints under Section 498A IPC even when reported after months or, in some cases, years. Rarely will women approach the police just days after marriage. If the woman reports harassment after months or years, it is understood that she has done so in an attempt to save her marriage and hoping that things would improve. But this is not the view taken by investigating officers when preparing the FRs under the SC/ST Act. It is not assumed that the victims might not have reported promptly fearing damage to their social lives and not wanting to antagonize the powerful upper castes.

Public-Private dichotomy and the different evidence standard

While Section 498A deals with the oppression in the "private sphere", the SC/ST Act is oriented towards the public sphere. The insult should have taken place "within public view". What constitutes the public? Is it only spatial? That the "personal is political" is accepted with respect to Section 498A but not with that to the SC/ST Act. It does not address the cumulative humiliation and mental agony that the SC/ST victim suffers day after day. This public-private dichotomy creates a special problem for them. The police apply a contradictory evidential standard. While relatives are understandably considered as valid witnesses in the 498A cases, even community members are considered as "interested" or biased witnesses under the SC/ST Act complaints. Sometimes the FR rests on the premise that all the witnesses were either relatives of the complainant or from the same community and are thereby "interested" parties. Though the law does not say that being a community member is tantamount to being an "interested" witness, the police construction of this theory depicts their unfriendly attitude and a mechanical investigative approach. They do not follow the "case to case" approach of the court which assumes that each case is unique.

Reconciliation

Both the laws are non-compoundable—the complainant cannot play a role in closing the cases. The justification in almost all the FRs under Section 498A rests on the complainant's purported desire for *rajinama* (reconciliation) presumably to save her family life, keeping the children in mind or because of her economic condition. The police almost seem to play a persuasive role in such situations. They are supposed to first try the reconciliation (legally, counselling) route before proceeding further in the 498A cases. The police legally categorize an FR under Section 498A containing *rajinama* as a "mistake of fact". Interestingly, about half such FRs under the SC/ST Act are categorised as "false" though they can very well be categorised as "mistake of fact" and save the complainant from possible legal sanction. The police even apply Sections 182 and 211 of the IPC for "lodging false cases" in some instances. This is an excerpt (translated from the Hindi) from an FR.

> (6) the matter is that complainant Modaram and his father Dayaram presented a jointly written *rajinama* wherein it was written that *rajinama* has been effected between both parties and do not want any further legal action. In this way this case was registered falsely by depicting imaginary facts by complainant Modaram taking help of lawyers to harass Mahesh Kumar and his family. This case is found totally false.

The issue of *rajinama* brings out the relation between the society and law. While the victim can take 498A to its logical conclusion by being prepared to walk out of the marriage, this is difficult in the SC/ST Act case as the victim has to continue living in the village or community. Members of the SC/ST are dependent on the upper castes socially, politically and economically. Many a times this could be the reason that the victims enter into *rajinama*.

False cases: Occasionally, even the judiciary has expressed apprehensions and warned about the misuse of Section 498A and the SC/ST Act. The general discourse among the upper castes and men is that these laws are largely misused. However, the reality is a little different. The words "health (whether mental or physical)" in Section 498A clearly imply that mental/psychological violence is well within the ambit of the law. Many acts can be construed as violent in the domestic sphere. For example, taunts (*taane marna*). Therefore, when a woman files a case under Section 498A months after the marriage has taken place, it is nearly impossible to say that no psychological violence could have happened as the definition of psychological violence rests with her and the scope of psychological violence is vast. The Supreme Court has observed that

> ...mental cruelty varies from person to person depending on the

> intensity or sensitivity and the degree of courage or endurance to withstand such mental cruelty (Kothari 2005, 4845).

However, sometimes the ulterior motive overrides any supposed psychological violence. A few FRs point out that it is a property issue or material interest that can give rise to the misuse of Section 498A. However, often, the wife acts only as a proxy for her husband who wants to gain materially from his father or brother. For example, according to one FR, the complainant, her father and her husband jointly defrauded the complainant's father-in-law of his land. The latter lodged a complaint in the Tuni police station (name changed). The woman's complaint was in retaliation.

While property issues can result in the misuse of Section 498A, many a time the use of members of the SC/ST as proxy by the upper caste to settle score amongst themselves can result in the misuse of the SC/ST Act. The SC/ST members are often dependent on the upper castes for their livelihood and they prefer to fall in line. Nearly 10 per cent of the FRs studied mention that upper-caste persons had cajoled and coerced a dependent SC/ST member to file a complaint against another upper-caste member in order to settle scores. The following is a translated excerpt from an FR.

> The investigations found that complainant Gajaram did not accompany Mahendra Singh in the tractor on the day of the incident. Lawyer Mahendra Singh got Gajaram to file a false case under the SC/ST Act to take revenge for the altercation with Kaluram Dewasi on account of his autorickshaw creating obstacle for his (Mahendra Singh's) tractor. Kaluram reiterated the same when questioned. The matter is found to be totally false and without any basis after complete investigation.

Interestingly, no FRs among the ones studied recommended that Sections 182 and 211 of the IPC should be applied against the upper-caste abettor in spite of concluding that he was the instigator (legally abetted). This too shows the caste bias among the investigation officers.

Conclusions

The prevailing discourse is that women and members of the SC/ST misuse Section 498A and the SC/ST Act, respectively. This discourse refuses to look at the possibility that men and members of the upper castes can misuse these laws by using women and SC/ST members as proxies. There is an urgent need to correct this misconception.

NOTES

1. *Economic & Political Weekly* XlIX, No. 41, (2014): 17-20.
2. National Commission for Scheduled Castes (2004-05): "First Annual Report", http://www,ncsc,nic,in/pages/view/219/218-first-annual-report Accessed on April 2, 2014.
3. False is a subcategory of final report, for example "Type of Final Report Unoccurred" in the studied state are following—"false", "mistake of fact", "mistake of law", "non-cognisable", "civil nature".
4. The percentage is derived from the ratio of total "Final Report submitted" plus "declared false" out of total of "charge sheeted", "declared false" and "final report submitted". The percentage is not derived from the total of current registered and previous year pending as many also remain pending at the end of the year. So, the total of charge sheeted, declared false, and final report submitted represents the total number of cases investigated in a year.
5. http://ncrb.nic.in/, Accessed on April 9 2014.

REFERENCES

Kothari, Jayna, 'Criminal Law on Domestic Violence—Promises and Limits'. *Economic & Political Weekly* 40, No. 46 (2005): 4843-4849.

Saxena, K.B., *Report on Prevention of Atrocities Against Scheduled Castes.* Delhi: National Human Rights Commission, 2002.

The Centre for Women Studies, *Report on Use and Misuse of Section 498A-IPC*, Jaipur: Rajasthan University, n.d.

15

Lacking the Basics: The Supreme Court Judgement on Atrocities Act[1]

There is a saying—'mastery is mastery of the basics'. The supreme court judgement on Atrocities Act (*Subhash Kashinath Mahajan v The State of Maharashtra*, 2018) reminds one of the saying. The adage 'mastery is mastery of the basics' is applicable to all disciplines including statistics and jurisprudence. This judgement was an interaction between statistics and jurisprudence. When an exercise involves the interaction between statistics and jurisprudence then the basics involved in both disciplines have to be taken into account. I will point out the basics of statistics and jurisprudence that are missed in this judgement.

Basic 1—In statistics only comparables can be compared with

One cannot compare apple with cabbage. Similarly, one cannot compare statistics belonging to one phenomenon with that of another. There are a couple of statistics related to the various stages in the justice process. For each stage, there is a comparable alternate stage and the statistics of both can be compared with.

One can see from table 15.1 that statistics pertaining to one stage of the justice process cannot be compared to statistics pertaining to another/next stage because one stage is very different from another/next stage. The level of scrutiny increases as we move from FIR to conviction/acquittal. Therefore, it is far-fetched to club final report (false cases)

Table 15.1: Statistics Pertaining to Stages in Justice Process

	Stages	Comparable alternate stages
1	FIR (First Information Report)	Victim reported crime/crime unreported
2	Charge sheet	Final Report (False Case, Civil Nature etc.)
3	Conviction	Acquittal

with acquittal rate. If one assumes false case on the basis of final report, then can one assume true case on the basis of charge sheet! If presumption of innocence holds at the stage of charge sheet then it holds equally well at the final report stage because both belong to a pre-trial mutually alternate stage.

Basic 2—You cannot rely on a statistic where just one case contributes more than 50 per cent of the total value

It is one state, Rajasthan, that is predominantly responsible for the false cases if we see *Crime in India 2016* published by the National Crime Records Bureau.

Table 15.2: Contribution of Rajasthan to False Cases

	India (all states)	Rajasthan	Percentage contribution of Rajasthan to India
False cases under POA[1] & PCR[2] for SC (Table 7A.4)	5347	2632	49.22
False cases under POA & PCR for ST (Table 7C.4)	912	612	67.10
When data on SC & ST combined	6259	3244	51.82

(Notes 1. Scheduled Caste and Scheduled Tribe (Prevention of Atrocities) Act, 1989; 2. Protection of Civil Rights Act 1955)
Source: http://ncrb.gov.in/StatPublications/CII/CII2016/pdfs/NEWPDFs/Crime%20in%20India%20-%202016%20Complete%20PDF%20291117.pdf. Accessed on July 30, 2018.

As Table 15.2 shows, if Rajasthan contributes about 52 per

cent of the total false cases, then the obvious analysis is that the issue of false cases is basically a Rajasthan issue and not an all-India issue. Here the basic the court missed is the query why the rate of false cases is so high in Rajasthan and not so in nearby Uttar Pradesh!

Basic 3—Statistics that do not reflect the phenomenon are not valid

These days sometimes the children have more expensive cell phones than their parents. This doesn't mean they have more money than their parents. Therefore, measuring people's financial worth by looking solely at their smart phones is not valid. The research proposals of MA students in social sciences customarily have a small section on issues of reliability and validity. Validity is about whether something is the right measurement device for the phenomenon under question; for example, you cannot measure temperature with metre or foot but with Centigrade or Fahrenheit. The issue before the court was the magnitude of false cases. What is the correct statistic to represent this? The valid statistics would have been the conviction rate under section 182 IPC for false cases for invoking Atrocities Act. The court relying on the acquittal rate instead of conviction rate under 182 IPC has totally missed the point.

Basic 4—In common law "It is better that ten guilty persons escape than that one innocent suffer"

While the court has quoted one of the basic principles of common law—presumption of innocence till proved guilty—it forgot another basic principle enunciated by Blackstone, "It is better that ten guilty persons escape than that one innocent suffers". If we accept this literally, then we have to be satisfied with a conviction rate of slightly less than 10 per cent. the correct interpretation of low conviction and high acquittal rate is that many guilty are still escaping without being convicted because of the benefit of the doubt given to them and the burden of proof placed on the accuser rather than the accused. This flows from a basic understanding of common law jurisprudence. If one remembers this principle then one cannot pass any comment on SC/ST lodging false cases on the basis of high acquittal rate.

NOTE

1. *Round Table India*, 31 July 2018, http://roundtableindia.co.in/index.php?option=com_content&view=article&id=9427:lacking-the-basics-the-supreme-court-judgement-on-atrocities-act&catid=129:events-and-activism&Itemid=195.

16

Misconstruction of the Anti-Atrocities Act's Misuse[1]

It is generally supposed that the legal proposition is to be accepted not because of *ratione imperii*, but *imperio rationis* (not by reason of power, *but* by power of reason). Pierre Bourdieu points out that it is difficult to find pure reason or pure power. Therefore, sometimes, people have to obey the court for the simple reason that they have to. The recent Supreme Court judgement (*Subhash Kashinath Mahajan v The State of Maharashtra* 2018) is the culmination of a discourse that portrayed the Scheduled Castes and Scheduled Tribes (Prevention of Atrocities) Act, 1989 (PoA) as more misused than used. The judgement in the case has relied on three other high court judgements (supposed to be illustrative and not exhaustive) and the National Crime Records Bureau's (NCRB) *Crime in India,* 2016 report. It does not quote any other government or academic study on the misuse of the act. If the NCRB data on false cases is proved to be irrelevant, which this article will try to do, then the judgement is relying on pure judicial acknowledgements. This is in stark contrast to the judgement on reservation in promotion (*M Nagaraj & Others v Union of India & Others* 2006) which in its conclusion emphasizes the importance of statistics.

> The State is not bound to make reservation for SC/ST in matter of promotions. However, if they wish to exercise their discretion and make such provision, the State has to collect *quantifiable data* showing backwardness of the class and inadequacy of

> representation of that class in public employment in addition to compliance of Article 335. (emphasis added)

False cases constitute a major part of the "final reports," popularly known as closed cases. This article draws from a study on the final report done for a state in north India. It was commissioned by the state government and accepted by its police department. The broad objective of the study was to investigate whether the final reports under the act are justified or not. It eventually turned into a study of false cases because out of the 498 cases studied (secondary data), 6.02 per cent were of a "civil nature," 3.41 per cent were classified as "mistake of fact" and about 89.36 per cent as "false." The author's analysis was based on primary and secondary data with the former comprising interviews of 76 complainants, 70 accused, and 69 witnesses pertaining to 73 final reports of 10 police stations in six districts. The secondary data analysis was based on around 500 final reports of all the police stations in the six districts. The reference year was 2010 with respect to four districts and 2013 with respect to two districts.

No Presumption of Innocence

As stated earlier, the supposed misuse of the PoA Act prominently hinges on the false cases category in the final report. A close look at the NCRB 2016 data that the Supreme Court judgement has relied on would be helpful (Table 16.1).

It is worth noting that when the figures under the Indian Penal Code (IPC) are compared to those under the act, the pattern in "false cases" is just opposite to that under "true but insufficient evidence." In the category of false cases, the IPC figure is 3.67 per cent while the act one is 13.58 per cent. In the category of true but insufficient evidence cases, the IPC figure is 19.86 per cent while that under the act is 4.92 per cent. How is this to be interpreted?

This article interprets these figures on the basis of the author's existing knowledge of the legal system. A police officer has pointed out that the rate of filing of charge sheets

Table 16.1 False cases and true but insufficient evidence—Comparison between Indian Penal Code and PoA

	Total Cases Disposed off by Police (Col 15)	False	False Case as % of Total Cases Disposed off	True But Insufficient Evidence	True But Insufficient Evidence as % of Total Cases Disposed off	Mistake of Fact	Mistake of Fact as % of Total Cases Disposed off
Total Cognizable IPC Crimes Table 17a.1	2874811	105546	**3.67%**	570941	**19.86%**	77353	**2.69%**
POA in conjunction with IPC (SCs) Table 7a.3	39577	5344	13.50%	2148	5.43%	867	2.19%
POA in conjunction wi th IPC (STs) Table 7c.3	6483	912	14.07%	119	1.84%	150	2.31%
When Data of SC and ST is Combined	46060	6256	**13.58%**	2267	**4.92%**	1017	**2.21%**

in a court of law is inversely proportional to the income of the accused (Saini 2000, 386). Another police officer has observed that "the Indian police have typical characteristics of being strong towards the weak and weak towards the strong (Gautam 1984). Therefore, the number of false cases under the IPC sections, which is caste neutral, appear fewer in comparison to those under the act, which deals with the weak and the marginalised.

The category of "true but insufficient evidence" basically provides a safe passage for the accused with the benefit of the doubt being given by the police. However, the police do not provide this escape route in PoA. This is the author's interpretation. If one goes only by the number of false cases without looking at the wider context, there is scope for sensationalism. For an example of this, one could say that there were 1,05,546 false cases under the IPC in 2016.

The registration of these cases can be seen as suspicion, the charge sheet as accusation and the judgement as conviction/acquittal. The false case in the final report is not even a suspicion, but the opinion of the police that a complaint is not true. It can be raised to the level of suspicion if the relevant IPC sections (182, 186, 211) are applied and action is recommended. Out of the 461 final reports in the study, a total of 47 (10.20 per cent) recommended application of the relevant IPC sections for lodging false cases. Theoretically, all cases labelled as "false" will attract these sections, though, in practice, the police in the cases studied imposed them on only about 10 per cent of the cases. If we take cognizance of these statistics, we have to virtually pare down the official statistics on the false cases by 90 per cent to get the true picture.

Be that as it may, if one is entitled to presumption of innocence even at the trial stage, then the complainant is fully entitled to the presumption of innocence at the stage of the false case in the final report. It must be emphasized that if presumption of innocence holds, the charge of misuse cannot hold.

In the study, each final report was classified as "justified," "not justified," or "inconclusive" after comparing the interview data of the complainant, accused, witness/es and the final report (the police record). "Justified" means that the police have rightfully concluded the final report, "not justified" means that they have not done so, and "inconclusive" means that it is not possible to comment based on the data available. Thus, "justified" does not mean that nothing happened but that there was no violation of "substantive justice." Sometimes, a wrong can be perpetrated while staying well within the right side of the law. There is a case in the study where a complainant's son abdicated his land in favour of the accused by signing some documents while under the influence of liquor plied on him by some persons and the lure of being taken to Italy. The police can do very little in such instances. There were 42 justified cases, 29 (39.72 per cent) not justified and only two were inconclusive. This implies that 40 per cent of the so-called false cases are themselves false. If we take this into account, we need to pare down the statistics of the official false cases in the final reports by 40 per cent to arrive at the correct number of false cases that deserve to be categorised as such. This also indicates that the power differential of the accused and complainant has a role to play in influencing whether a case is categorized as false or not. Finally, the study found seven cases of misuse of the act, meaning that the incident most probably did not happen at all. However, the complainant was a pawn for upper-caste rivalry in two cases. Therefore, if we assume that there were five cases of abuse of the act then the percentage is 6.85 per cent (five out of 73 cases of primary data).

Misuse by Upper Castes

The popularly accepted notion is that the PoA Act is misused by members of SCs/STs against the upper castes. There is as yet formally no acknowledgement that it is also misused by the upper castes to settle scores by using members of the SCs/STs as proxy. When the 461 final reports of six districts were analysed, 57 final reports (12.36 per cent) mentioned that the complainant was a pawn in upper-caste rivalry. While the relevant IPC sections were invoked against the complainant for lodging a false case in five different cases, no final report recommended any action against the "abettor."

The upper castes are able to misuse the law in two ways because of the imbalance of power between the upper castes and the SCs/STs. The former are entrusted with implementing the law. First, the complainant is put on the wrong side of the law. Second, the sheer weak position of the complainant forces them to allow the case to die. The first way is illustrated in the following cases (from secondary data).

> The complainant's father was allotted land in 1972 but did not occupy it as per the official records. The other villagers later on began opposing his occupation of the land on the ground that it had become "common land." There was no measurement of the plot by the revenue department when the road passed through this land.

One can easily imagine the situation, had the complainant been more powerful. On what basis could the villagers oppose the occupation of land allotted to him? If the government is responsible for constructing a road through the complainant's land without proper verification, then it should compensate him for the same. This is not a case where there is ambiguity of any kind. The police final report clearly mentions that the land belongs to the complainant, but it does not propose any proactive measure against the persons who are violating the complainant's rights. This indicates that the administrative structure mimics the bias present in the social structure.

The other feature of this imbalance of power is that, the victim, being in a weak position, cannot take a strong stand against the accused. The following case (from primary data) is illustrative of this.

> Complainant Subhash Jatav says— "While I was doing my work as a sweeper on January 3, 2013, Bhamma s/o Gajendra of the village came and said—*sale bhangi*, you do not sweep properly. Then I said—I do properly. Got angry on this and said—*sale bhangi*, dare to rebut me. Started assault on this—*sale bhangi*, got to drive you out from the village. Will close your source of livelihood and close the way to take the animals for grazing."
>
> Witness Shyam—"When Subhash was doing the sweeping work on January 03, 2013 then Bhamma s/o Gajendra of the same village assaulted and insulted with caste slurs. Fault was

> not of Harijan. All influentials of the village got together and harassed that poor a lot."
>
> Police Final Report—"Panchayat decided that all encroachment around *pokhar* to be removed. In this process complainant's hut was also removed. Complainant too submitted a *rajinama*."

Even if one takes the police version to be correct, one can guess that the victim may have encroached because he did not have land of his own. The police washed their hands off the case by pointing out the legally wrong position of the complainant. It is a no-win situation for the victim. If the victim wins on the legal front, they lose on the economic side, which they can ill afford. Winning is simply not an option. There is a legal proverb that states, "Let justice be done even if the world perishes." However, ordinary mortals can ill afford to perish and the need to live takes precedence over any other concern like justice. Therefore, directly or indirectly, the case is allowed to collapse. They might have the "ability to register" a case, but they do not have the "ability to pursue" a case because they are too vulnerable.

Voluntary/Involuntary *Rajinama*

Legally speaking, the *rajinama/samjhauta/samjhaic* "compounds" the case, though the PoA Act is "non-compoundable." This is also cited as some sort of evidence of misuse with the assertion that if it is true no one would compound it without considering the possibility that one may be forced to do so.

Out of the 461 final reports of the six districts, 81 (18 per cent) mentioned the *rajinama*, albeit in different ways explicitly and implicitly. In 11 cases, the IPC sections related to false cases (182, 186, 211) were recommended. As per primary data, 15 out of 71 cases (21.21 per cent) resulted in *rajinama*. Among the "not justified" cases, it was 27.58 per cent (eight out of 29). *Rajinama* per se may not constitute injustice, though it is illegal considering that the act is non-compoundable. But, *rajinama* under duress is both illegal and unjust. The *rajinama* in the "not justified" cases is a matter of concern. About 27.58 per cent *rajinama* cases are suspect. They are most probably under duress. The following statements are illustrative:

(i) "I did the *rajinama* on being told to do so by the villagers."

(ii) "The Deputy Superintendent of Police (DySP) came to appraise of the situation and got me to sign on the *rajinama* paper. He had come after *rajinama* ... (Justice is) equal treatment to all. No injustice to any."

(iii) "The *rajinama* in my case was not justice in my eyes but I signed on it because the village people suggested that I do so."

The principal reason why *rajinama* takes place is because of the persuasion cum pressure by other villagers, the elderly (*maziz*) in the village, the *sarpanch* and sometimes even the police. There is also the compulsion "to stay in the village." The weak and powerless complainant is in a double jeopardy situation when they are forced to do the *rajinama* under pressure and on top of it get charged under IPC Sections 182, 186, 211 for lodging a false case.

If upper castes can bend and twist the very law that is supposed to check their atrocity and put the SC/ST in a double jeopardy situation through forced complaint or *rajinama,* then how far is it tenable to constrain the act?

Compensation as Inducement

Overall, taking into account all the complainants, accused, and witnesses, only 42.31 per cent were aware of the PoA Act. What is a cause for concern is that complainants who primarily gain protection under this law, are not any more aware (37.84 per cent) than the accused (45.71 per cent). Only one complainant mentioned about compensation. Let alone the law, often the marginalised do not know about the fate of their cases, with about 45 per cent of complainants in the "not justified" cases being in this situation. If all the complainants are taken into account, 35.21 per cent are unaware that their cases have already become final reports.

If only 37.84 per cent of the complainants in the studied cases are vaguely aware of the law and if only one mentions compensation, then one has to doubt the assertion that compensation is a factor triggering false cases under this act. By lodging false cases, members of SCs/STs may or may not get compensation but they will certainly incur the wrath of the upper castes on whom they are dependent on many fronts. We have already seen that one of the reasons for *rajinama* is the "need to live in the same village."

Implication of prior permission

This study found that the first choice, whether voluntary or forced, is to register a case through the court (CrPc 156[3]). There is hardly any case registered through the superintendent of police's office. Roughly, only one-third of the cases are lodged in a police station, while the remaining two-thirds are registered through the court. Altogether, out of the 442 cases analysed, 70.6 per cent were registered through the court (CrPc 156[3]), 34.39 per cent were registered through the police station, and only 4.3 per cent were registered through the superintendent of police's office. This indicates the distance between the people and the superintendent of police's office.

The 10-year average number of cases in the study district ranged from 84 to 461. The senior superintendent of police (SSP) has a busy schedule. It is, thus, difficult to visualize the SSP being able to act with due diligence before giving or withholding the arrest order. In any case, the PoA Act does not have any specific guidelines regarding arrest. It does not say that arrest is a must if a first information report has been filed. Making prior approval of the SSP necessary can result only in delaying the procedure just like the earlier committal procedure was used to delay the cognizance by the sessions court.

Conclusions

So long as caste prevails, casteism and caste atrocities will continue. The Constitution has of course abolished untouchability through Article 17. However, it did not abolish the caste system, though it is the cause of untouchability. The caste system is justified by the Hindu scriptures like *Manusmriti* and the *Rig Veda*. These scriptures, which are an essential part of the Hindu religion, are protected under the freedom of religion granted in the Constitution. Stratificatory devices like caste, class, gender and ethnicity are also identities and the identity is a prized possession of individuals while being protected under a liberal framework, which is in turn based on individualism. Since one cannot abolish all the actual and potential stratifier-cum-identities (liberalism will never allow this), the next alternative is to remove the sharp edges of the stratifiers that hurt people. For this purpose, the rule of law devises various legal measures and the PoA Act is one such measure. Instead of putting a brake on this anti-discrimination law, there is an urgent need for taking legal measures against indirect discrimination, which is fully compatible with liberal constitutional morality.

NOTE

1. *Economic and Political Weekly* 53, No. 15 (2018): 11-14.

REFERENCES

Gautam, D.N., *What Is Wrong with Indian Police.* Delhi: NBO Publishers Distributors,1984.

M. Nagaraj & Others v Union of India & Others: WP(C) No 000061-000061/2002, http://sci.gov.in/jonew/judis/28160.pdf.

—— (2006): Writ Petition (Civil) No 61 of 2002, Supreme Court judgement dated 19 October, http://sci.gov.in/jonew/judis/28160.pdf.

—— (2018): Criminal Appeal No 416 of 2018, Supreme Court judgement dated 20 March, http://sci.gov.in/supremecourt/2017/2 2086/ 2-2086_2017_Judgement_20-Mar-2018.pdf.

Saini, Kamal, *Police Investigations Procedural Dimensions, Law and Methods.* Delhi: Deep and Deep Publications, 2000.

Subhash Kashinath Mahajan v The State of Maharashtra: ANR.Crl.A No-000416-000416-2018, http://sci.gov.in/supremecourt/2017/22 086 / 22086_2017_Judgement_20-Mar-2018.pdf.

17

Removing Discrimination in Universities[1]

Rohith Vemula's suicide, one among the several instances of suicides of *Dalit* students in Indian universities, has received a fair amount of attention. The event has also generated a feeling of helplessness among *Dalit* rights activists.

The notification and subsequent enforcement of the Scheduled Castes and Scheduled Tribes (Prevention of Atrocities) Amendment Act, 2015 came just a few days after the incident. Even before the amendment, the act, popularly known as Atrocities Act, had the image of a "stringent" act. It is true that by introducing a presumption vide Section 8 (c) it removes the difficulty of proving caste motive in instances of violence. But the amendment does not remove the burden and standard of proof, which would still need to be "beyond reasonable doubt," on the complainant. Legally stringent laws are those which shift the burden of proof to the accused and follow a standard of "preponderance of evidence" than "beyond reasonable doubt." So, calling it "stringent" is unfounded, going by legal standards.

Addressing Indirect Discrimination

Modern institutions like universities are too smart to practise crude discriminatory practices like separate water pots for *Dalits* that happen in some rural schools (Sukumar 2008). The defining attribute of indirect discrimination (practised in modern institutions like universities) is that it counts substance than form and impact than intent. Indirect discrimination operates by acting on discourses like merit, rights, academic freedom/autonomy, academic excellence and accountability in the university system.

Without a law on indirect discrimination, discrimination can always recur in changed forms. This seems to be what is happening. While law mandates for a certain percentage of SC/ST (SC/ST) student intake, which the higher education institutions cannot disobey, the SC/ST students suffer in multifarious ways after admission for which the Atrocities Act has very little answer.

For example, faculty are granted autonomy in good faith regarding certifying student progress. A faculty supervisor has substantial autonomy to certify whether the research scholar is progressing or not based on which the scholar's fellowship is granted. However, should the faculty misuse such autonomy and discriminate against SC/ST students then a law on direct discrimination like Atrocities Act will be ineffective as in extreme situations the faculty will take recourse to "error of judgement."

It is analytically useful to be aware that an empirical action could be the exercise of both rights/autonomy as well as discrimination. According to Max Weber, a real action in contrast to an ideal one can simultaneously be *zweckrational* (goal oriented), *wertrational* (value oriented) and affective (emotional). Further, action also includes "failing to act." We can also draw from Talcott Parsons that a particular action can be universalistic or particularistic to various degrees and not be divided into watertight compartments. The various actions/inactions that happen in the university may not be purely "rational" but may be laced with some "affect" and "tradition." A student's definition of a "good" teacher and a teacher's definition of a "good" student may not be purely "rational" in the sense of an objective assessment. Formally neutral norms/practices like "grading" and "student feedback" can constitute substantively discriminatory practices in a university.

Direct discrimination can be isolated and prohibited with relative ease. However, when discrimination is mixed with various discourses like rights, autonomy and excellence then it is difficult to separate and prohibit. This is indirect discrimination. However, advances in human rights has resulted in a focus on the concept of indirect discrimination. Simply speaking, this means what you should not be doing directly, should also not be done indirectly under any pretext (Doyle 2007).

A law on indirect discrimination (Tobler 2008) tries to counter such discriminations under the garb of rights/ autonomy. It does not accept neutral sounding discourses like university discipline or academic quality at their face values. One has no option but to curtail the rights/autonomy proportionately to prevent discrimination beyond a point. Just like affluence leads to effluence, discretion leads to discrimination.

A "statistical test" can be used as proof to raise the level of scrutiny against indirect discrimination. This method goes beyond the usual "case to case" approach and tries to spot a pattern. If almost all those who have committed suicides in a particular institution are *Dalits*, or if almost all those who fail and are expelled from a higher education institution are *Dalits*, then all of these cannot be a coincidence. This scrutiny makes institutions responsible in cases of indirect discrimination.

Usually only commissions constitute crime from the legal point of view. Authorities become culpable for their "activity", not their "passivity." However, from the morality point of view both commissions and omissions are crime. A real "civil" society cannot sustain itself only with laws of commissions. Laws related to omissions are equally necessary. A law on indirect discrimination takes care of omission as it focuses on the result rather than the procedure per se. It focuses on the final justice rather than only the procedural justice.

Discrimination Audit of Organisations

While we need reactive measures like law, we also need a proactive measure for tackling discrimination at modern institutions. It is said that law comes after, not before the crime. So even a law on indirect discrimination will act only after the discrimination takes place. It necessitates taking some proactive measure, less crude than law, which can capture and prevent indirect discrimination which is sophisticated. A discrimination audit can fulfil such a function.

The present era is supposed to be the audit era. We have performance audit, gender audit, environment audit, social audit, etc. Academics are facing the danger of the "audit culture" in a neo-liberal era. However, the equivalent of social audit, which happens for development projects, does not exist in academics. Academics exhort the government and the corporate to adopt social audit, but shy away from it when it comes to themselves. Who will judge the judges? Today in academics we have enough of performance audit but not of discrimination audit, the equivalent of social audit.

Discrimination audit can create moral pressure on the institutions to be more proactive to be just. Though this may only serve a symbolic function, it will be seen to be a moral compass in society.

NOTE

1. *Economic & Political Weekly* 50, No. 6, 6 February 2016, web exclusive. https://www.epw.in/journal/2016/6/web-exclusives/removing-discrimination-universities.html.

REFERENCES

Doyle, Oran, 'Direct Discrimination, Indirect Discrimination and Autonomy'. *Oxford Journal of Legal Studies* 27, No. 3 (2007): 537-53,

Sukumar, N., Living a Concept: Semiotics of Everyday Exclusion, *Economic and Political Weekly* 48, No. 46 (2008): 14–17.

Tobler Christa, Limits and Potential of the Concept of Indirect Discrimi-nation. European Commission, 2008. Http://Ec, Europa, Eu/Social/Blobservlet?Docid=1663&Langid=En Accessed on July 26, 2016.

18

Law and Exclusion

Can we think of something like 'inclusive law'? No, because it never strikes us. The law by definition is supposed to be inclusive. When other spheres like 'social' perpetrate exclusion, the law is supposed to rescue. But trajectory of the exclusion of the marginalised by law happens during law's formation, its various manifestations in terms of general and special laws and its operation. Thus, exclusion by law is an issue that one has to be constantly vigilant about. This article attempts to elaborate this with reference to the Scheduled Castes and Scheduled Tribes.

Law and inclusion can be discussed only within a particular legal system

Whether law is inclusive or not can be discussed only in a particular legal system. The same category of people who are afforded protection by the law in one legal system may be criminalized by another legal system. During colonial times certain tribes were "criminal" by law who now are not. Emile Durkheim made an important point when he said that we abhor crime because it violates collective conscience, and not because there is something intrinsic about it. Something is a crime because it violates collective conscience and not the other way round—the abhorrence because it is crime. This makes the definition of crime relative to time and place. That's how prostitution can be a crime in one era and society and not in another era and place. Homosexuality is a crime in one society and not in another.

Exclusion during formation of the type of legal system (constitution): liberal-bourgeois vs socialist

> ... the general interest includes protection of the social order against individuals who are beyond the pale of society. This protection may be effected by means of a part of the criminal law, police law, and procedural law. In reality all of this is a matter of the distribution of power (Ehrlich 2002, 198).

A legal system flows from a constitution which almost always is written. Whatever maneuver that a legal system can do is ultimately circumscribed by the constitution. Often people blame the legal system for not having the right type of laws without being aware that the constitution puts a limit to what type of laws can be made. Law and Versteeg (2011) in their empirical study demonstrate the ideological character of national constitutions. For example, constitutions can be characterized as relatively Libertarian, Socialist, or Islamist.

Drawing from a Marxist perspective legal systems can be divided into two types—the bourgeois-liberal and the socialist. Both bourgeois-liberal and the socialist legal system emphasizes rights, but of different types because of their underlying value premises. A socialist system, following Marx, considers private property as the root cause of the problem of society and therefore does not extend any protection to it. The premise of a socialist system is that the individual exists not only for herself but for the society as well and will find her fulfillment through the society. It emphasizes substantive freedom in the form of economic rights—"the right to work". Legal system is adjusted to ensure this. One consequence is that formal individual liberty is curtailed to the extent necessary to achieve substantive freedom in the society. The erstwhile USSR had such a system (Towe 1967). However, after the collapse of USSR and Chinese embrace of the market (Harvey 2005) today what we have in the world is various versions of liberalism with its various degrees of emphasis on the 'social'. Today when we talk of law and exclusion our default reference is a bourgeois-liberal law because the question of social exclusion arises only in a context which puts a premium on the individual and not social.

As the name suggests a bourgeois-liberal law emphasizes the sanctity of individual liberty, autonomy and privacy. The individual does not exist for the state but the state exists for the fulfillment of the individual. It is based on a negative conception of liberty (absence of any hindrance) rather than a positive conception which emphasizes substantive freedom. Right to property reigns supreme in a bourgeois-liberal system as a necessary corollary to individual liberty/autonomy/privacy. Bourgeois-liberal law considers right to property as second most crucial right next to liberty. The legal system is designed to ensure this. A classic example will be like the following. There are two persons, one having sufficient food while the other is hungry for days. In a bourgeois-liberal law it is not a crime for the first person with the food not sharing with the other. But it is a crime for the person without the food to snatch from the person having surplus food. This illustrates the sanctity of the private property (the food) to the exclusion of the social obligation (the obligation to share with the have-not). On the other hand, a socialist approach will not consider it a crime to take some food from the first and give it to the second.

The Indian Constitution and Exclusion

Constitution on paper and constitution in action is differentiated by designation of terms like "large C". and "small c". The Indian constitution is basically a bourgeois-liberal constitution. The adding of the word "socialist" cannot make it socialist in a reasonable sense just like the adding up the word "secular" cannot make it secular in a reasonable sense. Originally the constitution did have the "right to property" which was later abolished. However, by merely abolishing a particular fundamental right cannot alter the overall architecture of the constitution which remains liberal. For example, a law that takes away wealth from the existing wealthy people and gives it to poor is most likely to be struck down by the Supreme Court as violating individual freedom. The Supreme Court draws its supreme position from the constitution and therefore unlikely to strike at the root of "freedom" to promote socialism or social justice. Thus, in the Indian constitution social justice still has to come without violating too much the individual freedom.

Some are under the wrong impression that the Indian constitution has abolished caste. This impression arises due to conflating caste with untouchability which the Indian constitution has abolished (Article 17). Caste draws its legitimacy ultimately from *Rig veda*—probably the most sacred Hindu scripture. Hinduism as a religion is protected under Article 25 of the Indian Constitution. Therefore, abolishing caste, which entails destroying the authority of *veda* is difficult. Caste endogamy, which promotes casteism, is not an offence under the law. The fetish of endogamy sometimes leads to the so called honour-killing when a high caste girl marrying a low caste man is killed by her own relative/s. This is how the constitution with a liberal framework is not able to fully establish social inclusion.

Exclusion in the general and special laws

Constitution involves broad principles and values which are given detailed shape by the statutory laws. Law in general can be divided into material and procedural. In case of India the IPC (Indian Penal Code) is material law and the CRPC (Criminal Procedure Code), CPC (Civil Procedure Code) and the Indian Evidence Act are procedural. The laws further can be divided into general laws applicable to all and special laws to take care of particular sections of society. The IPC, the CRPC, CPC and the Indian Evidence Act are all general laws and the PCRA (Protection of Civil Rights Act, 1955) the SC/ST (Prevention of Atrocities) Act 1989 are examples of special laws.

It can be said that special laws are evidence of state's

seriousness to prevent exclusion. It is said that special law overrides general law, but the reality is that it happens mostly materially rather than procedurally. Thus, while most of the special laws are material in nature, they are still governed procedurally by the general law like the CPC, CRPC, and the Indian Evidence Act. This is something like the lack of "last mile connectivity" by dint of which the whole special law becomes infructuous. The question is whether such things happen by chance or by design by the dominant in the society.

For example, the SC/ST (Prevention of Atrocities) Act 1989 was enacted in 1989 but the Rules were framed as late as 1995, a good six years later. The rule contained directions to properly implement the Act like the constitution of vigilance committee at the district level, the compensation to be given to the victim etc. The requirement of *mens rea* under the general law was not exempted in the original SC/ST (Prevention of Atrocities) Act 1989 which always remained its Achilles heel. Thus, the accused, hailing from the same village could claim that he did not hurl insult keeping the caste of the victim in mind thereby indirectly claiming that he was unaware of the caste of the victim while hurling abuse. Obviously, an accused will never say that he has caste hatred in his mind. A special law like SC/ST (Prevention of Atrocities) Act 1989, without having measures to counter the procedural hurdles required under general law, is akin to lacking the last mile connectivity. This is how the law can exclude the marginalised while all the time claiming inclusion. This lacuna was removed by the SC/ST (Prevention of Atrocities) Amendment Act 2015 (1 of 2016)—26 years after the act was enacted in 1989. Section 8 (ii) (c) of the amended act reads: 'the accused was having personal knowledge of the victim or his family, the court shall presume that the accused was aware of the caste or tribal identity of the victim, unless the contrary is proved'. There was another Achilles heel of the SC/ST (Prevention of Atrocities) Act 1989. Originally the Act provided for the establishment of special courts at the level of sessions court for speedy trial of atrocity cases. But most state governments avoided the establishment of special courts by designating existing sessions courts as special courts for this purpose (Saxena 2002). Secondly, judges insisted that the exclusive or designated special courts cannot directly take up atrocity cases without being first committed by lower courts as required under section 193 of CRPC. The section reads, 'Except as otherwise expressly provided by this Code or by any other law for the time being in force, no Court of Session shall take cognizance of any offense as a Court of original jurisdiction unless the case has been committed to it by a Magistrate under this Code.' It's not the case that this section has no rationale. Since the Session Court is court of appeal from lower courts, cases should not go there at the first instance. However, in case of the SC/ST (Prevention of Atrocities) Act 1989 the legislature had provisioned for Special Court since the normal procedure would have resulted in delay. The logic behind this provision could be that the case is decided speedily at the highest district court so that it is fairly settled at the first instance, the next instance being the high court. This is in line with another feature of this act that the IO (Investigating Officer) in case of SC/ST (Prevention of Atrocities) Act 1989 has to be not below the rank of DySP, again at a higher level than in case of other IPC crimes. The legislature could not have intended the normal delay by the committal of the case to a sessions court. However, the Supreme Court in *Ashok Ganguli v. State of Andhra Pradesh* opined that the special court is essentially a session court which cannot take direct cognizance without following section 193 CrPC—committed to it by the magistrate (Qazalbash 2013). Two points are noteworthy in this regard. First, courts could have interpreted it less technically considering the ends of justice, and intention of the legislature in mind. The only function of the committal procedure was to delay rather than any positive function. Since cases under the PoA has to be tried not below the sessions court, the magistrate could not try it. The magistrate merely had to ritually commit it to the special session court whenever it comes before it. Second, the legislature could have corrected this anomaly at the earliest. However, this anomaly was corrected only in 2015 in the SC/ST (Prevention of Atrocities) Amendment Act 2015 (1 of 2016). Section 14 (I) of the amended act reads: 'provided further that the court so established or specified shall have power to directly take cognizance of offenses under this Act'. It took 26 years to add this vital sentence! This speaks about the willingness of the dominant section of the society to enact proper laws properly. Generally speaking, it is a long journey of decades from 'on the ground of untouchability' in the 'Protection of Civil Rights Act 1955' to 'on the ground of SC/ST' in the SC/ST (Prevention of Atrocities) Act 1989. It is easier to prove SC/ST (by furnishing a certificate) than untouchability.

A general feature of Indian legal redress mechanism is the adversarial system. Following common law system of UK, Indian legal redress mechanism adopts an adversarial system of procedure. Common law has an in-built tilt in favour of the accused. Blackstone was supposed to have said, 'It is better that ten guilty persons escape than that one innocent suffers'. That's why the benefit of the doubt always goes to the accused and not the complainant. This is the main reason of low conviction rate which gives the signal to the potential offender that punishment is unlikely. The number of laws of strict liability is kept to the minimum and these are reserved rather for crime against the state (representing the dominant) rather than crimes flowing from the social structure.

Be that as it may, the smartest way of discrimination and exclusion in a liberal society is the indirect way and not the direct way. Exclusion is mixed up with individual autonomy to make it difficult to separate and prohibit. This will be illustrated by the case of marriage. Caste system sustains through endogamy. However, the state cannot prescribe who to marry and who not to marry though a girl's acceptance or rejection of potential marriage partner may be based on caste consideration. Often it is brazenly mentioned in the marriage advertisements that SC/ST are simply not welcome as potential partners. The net result is that caste system and consequent stigma of lower castes continues through endogamy. This is how individual autonomy sustains social exclusion. The dilemma is, to what extent individual autonomy to be curtailed to promote social inclusion! Thus, a bourgeois-liberal law, standing guard for individual autonomy, may be a significant hurdle for social inclusion. Exclusion is perpetrated in the name of individual choice and autonomy. Marginalised groups are excluded from civic intercourse. They are prevented in an indirect way from housing ownership, rental market, club, jobs in the private sector etc. While there is a vibrant legal discourse and laws redressing indirect discrimination in the west (Tobler 2008), there is yet to be even an academic discussion about it in India! It is impossible that Indian elite will be unaware about the legal developments in the west. But the lack of discussion of such remedy shows the elite apathy to provide suitable legal remedy for the marginalised.

Chalabi (2014) points out that there are five ways rights can be restricted though every country professes to honour human rights by its law. The 5 ways are: (1) The frame of reference (2) The scope of rights (3) The orientation of rights (4) The enforceability of rights (5). The realizability of rights. For example, Hinduism as religion remains as a frame of reference in the Indian legal system. Buddhism and Jainism which arose as revolt against Hinduism are lumped with Hinduism by the law and the court. Cow, to the exclusion of any other animal, finds a mention in the constitution. This has now a devastating impact on the lives of lower castes and Muslims due to laws banning cow slaughter. This violates their right to life by violating their right to food and occupation.

Exclusion in implementation

The best of a racing car cannot move without fuel. It is better to have an ordinary car with fuel rather than a racing car without fuel. Proper implementation of general laws is much better than stringent special laws without the wherewithal and will to implement it. Exclusion happens through lax implementation of laws for the marginalised. The Elayaperumal Committee was constituted to evaluate Untouchability Offences Act 1955 and suggest measures to improve it (Government of India, Department of Social Welfare 1966). The report was submitted in 1969 but the Government did not bring up the issue in the House (Lok Sabha) until 1972. The Committee brought out how the lax implementation of the Untouchability Offences Act 1955 rendered it toothless. The Untouchability Offences Act 1955 came into effect from June 1955. The home ministry had written in June itself to all the states to form small Committees at headquarters to monitor the implementation of the act. The Elayaperumal Committee found that no state had formed committees except Bihar and Madhya Pradesh. But the governments of these two states did not act at all on the recommendations of these committees. The Act was not discussed in any of the state level advisory boards for *harijan* welfare whose job was it to recommend measures for *harijan* welfare. Secondly, while the home ministry advised the state governments to form committees to oversee the implementation of this act, it did not form any committee itself.

No exercise was done to publicise the Act. Andhra Pradesh, Bihar, Gujarat and Jammu & Kashmir simply did not publish the Act. Odisha published 500 copies of the Act in 1961 and Rajasthan published 2,000 copies in Oriya and Hindi respectively but they did not distribute at all. Tamil Nadu published 250 copies in Tamil but sold it to public on payment of cash. The Elayaperumal Committee found that even government servants were not aware about the Act. Out of 30 police officials, 27 were aware that untouchability is prohibited by the constitution, 15 (55 per cent) were aware of the Untouchability Offences Act 1955, but only 2 (7.5 per cent) were aware about the major provisions of the act. It mentions a peculiar instance:

> it was reported by Sri Avanta Mahapatra that at Bhanpur near police station the Scheduled Caste [persons] were to hold a meeting. The tea stall holder was requested to serve tea to the Scheduled Caste persons who had gathered there but unfortunately, he refused to do. Shri Mohan Nayak Ex MP who happen to be there went to the police station to lodge a complaint under the Untouchability Offences Act 1955 but to his great surprise the assistant sub inspector said that he could not register the case as he was not aware of the various provisions of the Untouchability Offences Act 1955. This shows the apathy and ignorance of the police officers in understanding the problems of the Scheduled Castes (Government of India, Department of Social Welfare 1966, 24-25).

Theoretically, to say that an ASI has good knowledge about the law is to denigrate top lawyers and judges who are supposed to have in depth knowledge about law. However, what action can be taken against an ASI who can take the pretext of ignorance! He could have tried to find out. These are nothing but novel ways of denying justice to the marginalised.

However, the ultimate master stroke of the dominant is to drive a wedge within the marginalised co-opting a section of it. Elayaperumal complained unequivocally about the non-cooperation extended by the very Social Welfare Department which was to facilitate the Report to the extent that he spoke of the "room being sealed" and the Committee had to operate from a residence towards the end. The non-cooperation of the government was evident by the fact that ultimately the department did not agree to include "service matters" within the scope of the Committee though Committee proceeded with the full knowledge of the government. Committee included service matters/employment in the final report as it considered the report would be meaningless without it. Also, while some state governments and PSUs (Public Sector Undertakings) gave data related to employment (service matters), the social welfare department itself did not provide such data to the Elayaperumal Committee. It is also significant that one Scheduled Caste member openly wrote against the

Committee saying that the principal problem is economic and not untouchability reminding of the present debate about caste vs economic criterion. The dissenting note of Shri R Achutan reads:

> I do not agree with the view of other members that there is an acute form of untouchability in UP and Gujarat, especially it is not true in view of the fact the *harijan* chairman and members of the committee while they were on tour in Gujarat lavishly enjoyed the hospitality of the *Brahman*s in Gujarat (ibid, VIII).

If one takes the two facts—the non-cooperation of the department and one Scheduled Caste member opining such outrageous opinion against the Committee whose chairman was a SC, then one wonders whether extraneous upper caste influences shaped the opinion of the dissenting SC member Achutan. One can smell the hand of the dominant section behind it. The reason given by Achutan, that Committee members complaining about untouchability in Gujarat by upper castes is unjustified when they are enjoying the hospitality of *Brahmans*, seem to be a reaction rather than a reason. With hindsight, Gujarat is the place most well documented about untouchability (Shah et al., 2006).

Exclusion by the legal actors

There are three important actors in the matter of justice—the police, the lawyer and the court. In the first instance, law is what the police says. Later, law is what the lawyer says and ultimately law is what the court says. If the law is a powerful machine then these actors are its drivers at various stages. The machine, though may be powerful, is powerless without these drivers. Thus, special laws, though designed to be powerful, can be implemented well or lackadaisically depending on the performance of these legal actors.

There is now a significant amount of sociological literature on police, many a time by retired high ranking police officials themselves which brings out the fact that people do not leave their biases flowing from their social moorings when they don the uniform. An ex-DGP (Director General of Police) opines that the Indian police have a typical characteristic of being 'strong towards the weak and weak towards the strong' (Gautam 1984). He has observed that police lines are patterned on caste lines. 'There is no wonder then that when it comes to the protection of rights of SC/ST and the OBC the administration and the police have been known to be inclined to act against the interest of the weaker section not only because of the influence of the social, economic and political power, but also on account of an existing natural bias among these operatives which determines the use of their discrimination' (Chande 1997, 323). The Indian police did not originate during the British period to provide social justices (Sarolia, Sarolia 2005). A continuation of this is that usually police officers are posted to civil rights units as a measure of punishment and they do not take their work seriously (Subramanian 2007, 167).

In contrast to the police, lawyers and judges have escaped sociological scrutiny in India. In principle, there is nothing which stops the SC/ST to engage a lawyer or a good lawyer. In reality a SC/ST wage laborer cannot engage a lawyer, forget about a good lawyer. In principle, the state is obliged to provide him merely a lawyer, not a good lawyer. The lawyer in turn is obliged only to do her job, but not to do her job well. This is how exclusion happens during the legal process. Empirical studies substantiate this. K.L. Sharma (1984) did a study of lawyers in Jaipur, Rajasthan. It found that the legal game, if it can be termed like that, was basically an upper caste game where the clients and lawyers both were overwhelmingly upper caste. Out of 140 lawyers, 51 were *Brahman,* 48 *Bania* and *Jain* and 17 *Kayastha.* Among clients, out of 125, 32 were *Brahman,* 26 *Bania* and *Jain* and 20 from intermediate castes. Caste linkage between clients and lawyers shows that 71 out of 125 clients had lawyers who hailed from their neighborhood, village area or belonged to their caste, community and some of them were also related to each other. There were 10 Scheduled Caste/Scheduled Tribe clients but no lawyer from the SC/

ST. These SC/ST were also those who had some connection with some influential persons. This means they were not the average, powerless SC/ST. All this shows how the traditional social stratification has been overlaid on a modern profession like the legal profession continuing the marginalisation of the traditionally marginalised.

Apart from lawyers, even the judiciary can shed their expected impartiality. The Elayaperumal Committee noted:

> it has however been brought to our notice from various quarters that some cases are deliberately delayed in order to subject the Scheduled Caste people to various hardships so that they may be tired out as a result of procrastination and may not be left with any energy and resources to contest the cases ... to illustrate it was reported to us that the trial of a case in Sinar taluka in Nasik district in the state of Maharastra was spread over a period of 2 years involving 27 adjournments, and on the 28th hearing the complaint was dismissed for the non-appearance of the complainant who by then was completely exhausted. It was also a unique feature of the case that during all these hearings the accused never appeared in the court (Government of India, Department of Social Welfare 1966, 51).

In another case the accused was fined only Rs. 3 even after admitting the guilt. In another case the judge declared 'the offense having been compounded out of court the accused are acquitted under section 325(b) CRPC' (ibid, 52). How witnesses can compound a case! K.L. Sharma (1984) too in his study found that clients believed that some judges are biased and have questionable integrity.

> The opinions of clients about magistrates varied vastly. They were either considered honest, competent or dishonest, corrupt or incompetent. Magistrates are not beyond the influence of the rich and the power elite. Delay is the most common weapon in the hands of the magistrate. Some of them do not understand the law properly and therefore some competent and clever lawyers secure the decision they want from them. Besides this the judiciary is not above the influence of caste, creed and community considerations since a good number of them belong

> to upper and upper middle-class families. The lower and the untouchable castes do not expect sympathetic dealings from them. From 90 statements it is apparent that magistrates are a highly differentiated category of people in respect of their social background, personal likes and dislikes, competence, honesty and dishonesty, hard work, personal character, integrity etc.... in case a client hesitates to pay or does not want to pay the concerned clerk the latter creates a series of obstacles for the client. These include the delay of work, misplacement of the file, getting postponement of the date and rude behaviour. The magistrates and other court officials know of the misdeeds of their clerks and it is alleged that some of the magistrates accept pecuniary or other material gratifications through their clerks (ibid, 94).

This shows how the court process can exclude the marginalised from justice. The court is supposed to be the house of justice. If the marginalised cannot get justice from there, then the last door of justice is closed for them. Discrimination flows from discretion. Biggest source of a judge's discretion comes from being allowed to play the game of "form" and "spirit" of a law—hold on to the form or spirit of the law as per his discretion. Judges are given discretion on the combination of punishment (imprisonment or/and fine) and range of punishment—upper and lower limit of punishment e.g 6 months to 2 years of punishment. These discretions of the judges are absolute by law and no question can be raised about their exercising such discretion.

Conclusion—the limitation of a legal category trying to represent a social phenomenon

The legal categories of Scheduled Castes and Scheduled Tribes have emerged historically to represent the most marginalised in the Indian society. However, the legal category based on executive fiat homogenizes the entire spectrum of Scheduled Castes and Tribes who vary in terms of education, economic and social status. It cannot adequately represent low, marginal and oppressed castes who cut across religions. The legal categories are used both for affirmative actions as well as protection of civil rights and prevention of atrocities. While it may make sense that state boundaries are fit for providing reservation benefits for education and jobs, it does not make sense for the purpose of protection of rights and providing justice. Since providing reservation benefits requires resources, presumably from the state, the criteria of geographical (state) and religious boundary may be reasonable. But protection of rights requires appropriate behaviour from everybody. Therefore, geographical (state) and religious boundary defining Scheduled Caste/Scheduled Tribe in case of criminal law is not reasonable. Therefore, while a restrictive meaning of Scheduled Caste/Scheduled Tribe can be applied for affirmative action, an expansive meaning cutting across geographical (state) and religious boundary should be used for criminal law to protect rights.

NOTES

1. *The Gazette of India Extraordinary*, January 18, 2016.
2. 2000, Cr. LJ 819 [SC]: AIR 2000 SC 740 : 2000 AIR SCW 279.

REFERENCES

Chalabi, Azadeh, 'Law as a System of Rights: A Critical Perspective'. *Human Rights Review* 15, (2014): 117–138.

Chande, M.B., *The Police in India*. Delhi: Atlantic Publishers & Distributors, 1997.

Ehrlich, Eugen, *Fundamental Principles of the Sociology of Law*. London: Transaction Publishers, 2002.

Gautam, D.N., *What is Wrong With Indian Police*. Delhi: NBO Publishers Distributors,1984,

Government of India, Department of Social Welfare, *Report of the Committee on Untouchability and Economic and Educational Development of Scheduled Castes* (L Elayaperumal, Chairman), 1966.

Harvey, David, *Brief History of Neoliberalism*. Oxford: Oxford University Press, 2005.

Law, David S. and Mila Versteeg, 'The Evolution and Ideology of

Global Constitutionalism'. *California Law Review* 99, No. 5 (2011): 1163–1174.

Qazalbash, Yawer, *Commentary on the SC/ST (Prevention of Atrocities) Act 198*. Delhi: Universal Law Publishing House, 2013.

Sarolia, Shankar and Gaurav Sarolia, *Perspectives on Indian Police*, Jaipur: Society for Development and Public Issues, 2005.

Saxena, K.B., *Report on Prevention of Atrocities Against Scheduled Castes*. Delhi: National Human Rights Commission, 2002,

Shah, Ghanshyam, Harsh Mander and Sukhadeo Thorat, *Untouchability in Rural India*. New Delhi: Sage Publications, 2006.

Sharma, K.L., *Sociology of Law and Legal Profession*. Jaipur: Rawat 1984.

Subramanian, K.S., *Political Violence and the Police in India*, Delhi: Sage, 2007.

Tobler, Christa, Limits and Potential of the Concept of Indirect Discrimination. European Commission, 2008. Http: / / Ec,Europa, Eu / Social / Blobservlet?Docid=1663&Langid=En Accessed on July 26, 2016.

Towe, Thomas E., 'Fundamental Rights in the Soviet Union: A Comparative Approach'. *University of Pennsylvania Law Review* 115 (1967): 1251-1274. Http: / / Scholarship,Law,Upenn,Edu / Cgi / Viewcontent, Cgi?Article=6224&Context=Penn_Law_ Review. Accessed on July 26, 2016.

Index